"EMERGE comes at a critical time for the green building commun
advances, but we lag behind in our ability to create deeper chan
will exercise leadership muscles we didn't know we had and bec

Lucia Athens, Chief Sustainability Officer, City of Austin

"What's amazing about this book is how Kathleen O'Brien has managed to pull together her decades of incredible experience into a cohesive and actionable book. Her model for leadership will transform how effectively you and your team work together, and re-focus your organization's mission to benefit the greatest good. Her innovative framework of "Leadership, Change, and Community" will provide you the tools you need to foster the emerging leaders on your team. This is a must read for anyone working with the built environment."

Eric Corey Freed, Architect & Author of "Green Building for Dummies" and 10 other books

"EMERGE will help you become a better leader. I wish this book had been around when I was getting into the renewable energy and green building fields in the late 1970s. I think I would have accomplished more and, more importantly, I suspect that the organizations I led would have been more effective."

Alex Wilson, Founder of BuildingGreen and the Resilient Design Institute

"O'Brien's Emerge is well worth reading for anyone who is trying to make a difference. Her target audience -- green building and sustainable development professionals -- will particularly appreciate the examples from practice, but the subject matter is equally relevant in other social endeavors. And rest assured that even if you find yourself accidentally, reluctantly, falling into leadership, this book is for you. Leadership is at the bottom of a slippery slope of caring and volunteerism: you might not have planned to end up there, but you still can and should be as effective as possible, because the world needs more good leaders!"

Ann Edminster, Architect, Author of "Energy Homes for a Small Planet"

"Kathleen has given a great gift to the green building community -- helping to take her considerable experience and leadership and begun to describe a coherent path forward around the paradigm of 'emergent leadership'. With compelling examples, personal reflections and case studies -- this book provides you with an opportunity to increase your effectiveness, reach and personal transformation both for yourself and for the others you serve as 'servant leader'. I recommend this book as a great thought piece on positive change."

Jason McLennan, Architect, Author, and Developer of the Living Building Challenge and related tools

EMERGE

A Strategic Leadership Model For
The Sustainable Building Community

Kathleen O'Brien

New Hope Press
Seattle, WA

For information, address
New Hope Press
321 High School Road, Ste D3 #715
Bainbridge Island, WA 98110
www.emergeleadershipthebook.org

Published 2016

ISBN 9780996997805

Library of Congress Control Number: 2015919318

Book Design by Suzanne Davis & Hillary Handy

To all those who work for the common good in caring for

our common home.

"The poor and the earth are crying out...
Help us protect all life to prepare for a better future."

- From a prayer offered by Pope Francis, May 2015

Table of Contents

Foreword
by Alex Wilson

I wish this book had been around when I was getting into the renewable energy and green building fields in the late 1970s. I think I would have accomplished more and, more importantly, I suspect that the organizations I led would have been more effective.

I've long thought of myself as an accidental leader. When I sat daydreaming in high school classes years ago – gazing out the window – the future I envisioned for myself was never to be leading anything or anyone. I figured I'd be a researcher studying aquatic ecosystems or maybe a writer sitting in a cabin off in the woods somewhere, penning insightful essays about nature, like my heroes John Muir or Ed Abbey.

But I somehow kept falling into leadership roles. In 1978, I was promoted from a VISTA Volunteer position with the New Mexico Solar Energy Association (NMSEA) in Santa Fe to lead the organization's four-person Workshop Crew. We traveled around the state leading hands-on solar workshops to teach people about solar retrofits by having them take part in building those systems. My title was leader of the program, but the four of us really ran it together.

After several years in New Mexico advancing solar energy, I was asked to consider the executive directorship position of a sister organization in Vermont, the New England Solar Energy Association (NESEA). In a fit of uncharacteristic bravado (likely fueled by a few beers), I agreed to apply for the position, and – even more remarkably – was hired. While I had participated in some administrative functions at NMSEA, I was a wet-behind-the-ears 25-year-old, woefully unprepared to run a regional nonprofit organization.

Just after assuming the leadership of NESEA in the fall of 1980, a new president was elected in Washington who not only removed the solar panels from the White House, but eliminated funding of the Regional Solar Energy Centers, upon which NESEA depended for half of its funding. As a result, I learned the hard way about certain aspects of leadership, such as dealing with budget deficits and letting staff go.

While there were certainly many bright spots during my tenure at NESEA, including hiring Kathleen O'Brien to edit our monthly newsletter in 1983, the leadership role was a challenge that I didn't particularly enjoy.

After five years as executive director of NESEA, I struck out on my own as a writer. To make ends meet in that difficult career, I took on technical writing projects for utility companies and state energy offices, and I found myself needing support. So I hired a few part-time staff. Again, I found myself in an accidental leadership role.

In 1992, with Nadav Malin, whom I had hired a year earlier, we decided to launch a newsletter focused on green building, Environmental Building News. It was the first publication of its type in North America, and we quickly gained a following of loyal readers. The company grew, and I was – reluctantly – at the helm, struggling to meet payroll, carry out strategic planning, and manage a growing staff. BuildingGreen, now under Nadav's leadership, is finally turning a profit.

Thinking back over this history makes me wonder how different my career might have been if I had learned more about leadership along the way.

I'm convinced this book would have made a big difference in my turn at directing NESEA and founding BuildingGreen, both in terms of organizational effectiveness and profitability and in terms of personal satisfaction. Whether or not you are setting out to be a leader, this book will benefit you in many unexpected ways. It doesn't matter if you've created an entrepreneurial venture to make the world a better place, or you're serving on the board of a local nature center, or you're just trying lead successful family outings on the home front – this book will help.

Leadership skills are important to everyone, especially those of us who want to make a positive difference in the world; Kathleen's book will help you become a better leader.

Alex Wilson is founder of BuildingGreen, Inc., and president of the <u>*Resilient Design Institute*</u>*, both based in Brattleboro, Vermont.*

Preface

In late 2011 after a 30-year career in the sustainable building field, I decided it was time to pass on what I'd learned about leadership through lived experience and scholarship. I'd learned through trial and error and study (I'm a crazy reader) that some things worked very well, some things not so well, and some things not at all. It seemed that this information would be useful to those entering and those continuing to work in the field, and I was moved to share it in some way. I determined I would put on one workshop – one. Some friends helped me with planning and marketing. We called it EMERGE and named this initiative The EMERGE Leadership Project.

As of this writing (2015), the Project has conducted 10 workshops, as well as seminars and presentations that in total have reached nearly 2000 individuals. The Project itself has evolved and is now a 501c3 non-profit, with fundraising capacity, and multiple offerings, including mentoring, organizational retreats and training, and a curriculum centered around a model – the EMERGE Leadership Model. Success stories of workshop participants and others exposed to the model and the EMERGE curriculum have convinced me that it's time to write a book, so more people in the field can benefit from this model and the story behind it. As I say elsewhere in the book, we have an urgent need to lead more effectively, and this is my contribution to that effort.

The EMERGE Leadership Project mission is to *energize the emergent leadership capabilities of green building professionals and sustainability advocates through training, mentoring, community engagement, and other support, with the ultimate goal of fostering a thriving and life-sustaining environment.* If you wish to learn more about what the Project is doing or support the work through a donation, you can do so at emergeleadershipproject.org. You can also write me at kathleen@emergeleadershipproject.org. I'd love to hear about your leadership work.

Introduction

I've been involved in the sustainable building field for more than 30 years, as an educator, writer, researcher, facilitator, strategic planner, and project manager. Throughout the years, I've been privy to the green building movement's ups and downs. I've seen solar panels and energy conserving features installed on the White House, removed, and installed again. I've seen construction and development activity ebb and flow, and with it green building activity. I've seen public awareness and support for green building ebb and flow as well, spiking especially during times of crisis, such as when natural or human-made disasters illuminate our tentative hold on a quality of life that in better times we assume is ours to keep.

In general, however, we've seen an increase over the last few decades in the support for and implementation of "sound" building concepts, whether they were called environmentally sensitive, green, resource-efficient, high performing, or healthy. But is sustainable building the norm? I think we can agree that it is not.

Yet, I hold dear a vision of a society in which a sustainably built environment *is* the norm, not an abstraction. To achieve this vision assumes the incremental progress we have made, though laudable, needs to be accelerated. We need a dramatic change in thinking and practice to do so. And, we need leaders to facilitate this change.

Given the urgency of our times, we need lots of leaders, and lots more effective ones. And given the complexity of the issues involved, we need these leaders to be working from multiple vantage points within and through our organizations, and at all levels of community. We cannot continue our simplistic reliance on leadership by charismatic celebrity, titled personality, and/or through legal force.

People can *learn* to be leaders, and they can lead "from *any* chair," through collaboration and persuasion. In fact, I believe a highly collaborative service-oriented approach to leadership is better suited to achieving lasting change and more aligned with the philosophy of sustainability. This more effective approach, in attempting to shape the complex built environment, with its many players, influences, and choices, is exactly what we need. It more aptly reflects the philosophy of sustainability because it takes into account all of the systems - environmental, social, economic - that come into play in creating a thriving sustainable world.

In this book, I'll be sharing a model of leadership that integrates aspects of leadership philosophy, change psychology, and community context that together provide a framework for the kind of systemic transformation I envision. In this transformation, *the built environment is both the result of and catalyst for a shift in mindset* that is urgently needed, and if achieved will go well beyond improving bricks and mortar.

I am assuming my readers are at least sympathetic with if not already convinced that a transformation of our built environment is necessary and good, that sustainability represents a positive future. Thus,

this book will not include arguments for the same, although I will clarify what I mean by "sustainability" and "transformation," just to make sure we are on the same page.

I will also assume the reader is considering or has already committed to taking a leadership role in regard to this transformation. I've developed the EMERGE Leadership Model to better articulate to potential "emergent" leaders that what I've learned over the course of my professional career works and has also been affirmed through study of "best practice" literature. The Model is intended to be "suggestive," not prescriptive, providing readers with a way to develop the mindset of an "emergent" leader. In addition to a philosophical framework, the book includes suggestions to help you develop and strengthen your "emergent" leader muscles and case studies to inspire you.

Even the most committed of us needs to know this really works. One aim of this book is to support that it really does!

Finally, although the book is primarily a guide for individuals working on some aspect of sustainability, I do provide some guidance on how an organization might foster emergent leadership.

Navigational Advice

It's best if you read this book from start to finish. It is intended to build on itself. And I've kept it short, well, because I know you! But I recognize this is a lot of content packed into a tight space. For that reason I've created bonus materials, including chapter enrichment resources, links, and reading recommendations. (See the Author's Final Note for how to access these materials.) You might want to check out the chapter enrichment resources – exercises and videos – as you complete each chapter to help you deepen your understanding as you go. But feel free to access these materials once you've read the entire book.

The chapters in the book contain sidebars, written by me, which are intended to highlight a particular idea pertinent to the chapter. The book also contains two other elements: Essays by colleagues that provide thoughtful commentary on particular topics, and Transformation in Practices (TIPS) or case studies which highlight projects or programs that exemplify the kind of deep transformation possible with emergent leadership. The Essays appear in Chapter 7, 10, 11 and 15. The six TIPS appear in the interstices between chapters.

Confessions of an Introvert

In late 2011, I had the satisfaction of entrusting my 20-year-old green building consultancy based in Seattle to three younger principals, plus nearly a dozen other employees. The firm was a pioneer in the field, being one of the first like it in the Northwest. And by the time I turned over the keys, we could boast of multiple successes. O'Brien & Company had been instrumental in the development of a dozen local green building programs in several states, resulting in more than 30,000 units of certified green buildings in the public and private sector. Our demonstration projects represented a wide variety of building types: grocery stores, city halls, schools, market rate homes and affordable housing projects, office buildings. In the early projects, the focus was a single-note, such as construction waste management or energy efficiency. In later projects, such as my own home, or when developing a multi-level green building program (e.g., Built Green®), the efforts were more comprehensive, aiming at multiple green building attributes.

These early-stage projects meant I was often in a very public role, facilitating groups made up of individuals with widely ranging opinions, knowledge bases, and skill sets. A public facilitative role was not my natural inclination. I had happily spent my earlier career as a journalist and researcher. But my curiosity got the best of me. I wrote an article in the early '90s pondering the question: "Given the varying definitions of green building, what is it really?" This question led to the suggestion that I (along with a lot of friends!) coordinate an educational event where the definition of green building was explored. The result was "Building With Value" in November 1993,

which, as far as I know, was the first conference focused on green building construction in the United States. The rest, as they say, is history.

For those of you who think that to be a leader you must be an extrovert, *I'm living proof that you don't*. Once, while participating in a train-the-trainers workshop sponsored by the Northeast Energy Efficiency Alliance, the leader conducted an exercise to determine where participants were on the extroversion-introversion spectrum. I ended up – alone – at the far end of introversion. Our workshop leader exclaimed, "What are you even doing here!?" I told her that I'd already been presenting to lots of audiences; I just didn't feel comfortable doing it. I needed help developing a style of training that worked for me. She suggested I stop trying to lecture, and start having conversations with "friendly" individuals in the audience. (It worked.)

In addition to facilitating projects with various stakeholders, I've enjoyed success developing and conducting professional educational programs. One such was the Sustainable Building Advisor (SBA) program. SBA students were getting a comprehensive review of the technical aspects of green building. But towards the end of my tenure leading the SBA program I began to think about leadership and the need to develop a community of leaders who could excel and support each other in that excellence.

By this time, I had received several regional leadership awards, earned a graduate level certificate in servant leadership at Gonzaga University, and incorporated leadership training at O'Brien & Company as part of employee development. As the above-mentioned 20-year anniversary for my company approached, a part of me – the introverted part – wanted to hike, write a memoir, spend more time with family. But the "cause" still called. So, yes, I am taking time to hike and hang with family, but a memoir? Not so much. In fact, hiking and spending time with my grandkids only makes the work seem more important. Instead I've developed the EMERGE Leadership Project and with this book expect to spend more time in front of people than ever!

Looking back, it's hard to believe that at age 10, I'd frown into any camera pointed my way, but I did. I share all of this to encourage you. If you're an introvert committed to a cause you believe in, you can become an effective and even comfortable leader, especially if you rely on the more *collaborative service-oriented leadership model* I present in this book. Being an introvert does not have to get in the way of being a leader – and it may even enrich your leadership style if you let it. And if you are an extrovert, I encourage you as part of your leadership to provide space for your introverted colleagues to lead.

What Is the EMERGE Leadership Model?

Emergence is the phenomenon in nature where simple(r) elements come together to form a functional and beautiful complex system. Emergence in nature is a perfect description of how the EMERGE Leadership Model came to be, as well as how I see this leadership taking shape within the individuals applying it.

Figure 2.1

When I first began presenting the emergent leadership approach to green building practitioners and advocates in late December 2011, I was simply offering my bucket of lived experience and study in three main topic areas: leadership, change, and community. (Figure 2.1) Within these topics, there were principles and practices. Workshop participants said the information was helpful...and I'm sure their feedback was based on what they've accomplished with it.

But it wasn't until January 2013, at a workshop at NatureBridge (Marin

LEADERSHIP

Figure 2.2

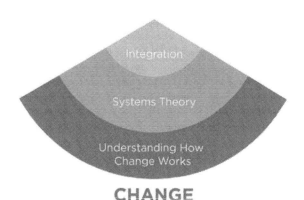

CHANGE

Figure 2.3

County) that the information all came together in the form of a model. You can thank my dear colleague, and EMERGE Faculty member, Ann Edminster, for that. During a group discussion of the overall approach, Ann grabbed a magic marker, a flip chart, and in the way only Ann can do, drew a model of the concept, and asked, with a flourish, "Isn't this what it is?" And of course it was. We've prettified the model (and created derivative illustrations that "parse" it), but basically the model is as Ann drew it that day. As you can see from the illustration on the previous page, the EMERGE Leadership Model consists of three components: Leadership, Change, and Community.

Each of the three components of the EMERGE Leadership Model is divided into tiers that I've named the *foundation*, the *centerpiece*, and the *distinction*. The foundation is the bottom line, if you will, the centerpiece is exactly as it denotes, and the distinction is the "cherry on top."

For the Leadership component, the foundational tier is: principled business practice; the centerpiece is servant leadership; and the distinction is aspiration. Emergent leadership is characterized by integrity, an attitude of service, and positive aspirations. (Figure 2.2)

For the Change component, (Figure 2.3) the foundational tier is: understanding how change works: the centerpiece is systems theory or thinking; and the distinction is integration. Emergent leaders understand that there are conditions for change to occur. As an emergent leader, you can foster those conditions. The integrative design process, for example, is a change management process, and can be used as a strategic leadership tool. Emergent leaders approach different situations freshly, understanding that to acquire positive change, the unique characteristics of each situation demand just that.

For the Community component the foundation is: collaboration; the centerpiece is learning; and the distinction is caring. An emergent leader practices what I like to call collaboration on steroids! But more importantly, the emergent leader understands that it is a delusion to think that he or she is leading alone, or that he or she even could. (Figure 2.4)

The Model is intended to suggest not prescribe. Prescriptive leadership formulas, e.g., "Five Easy Steps to Leadership Success," are by their very nature un-strategic and therefore limited in their value vis-à-vis addressing systems-based conditions. EMERGE provides a philosophical framework with embedded principles that if applied will help you develop your personal capacity to practice emergent leadership.

A frequently used example of emergence in nature is the snowflake – a wonderful example of a system that is beautiful, functional (water transporting itself), and unique. As with snowflakes, the leadership that emerges using The EMERGE Leadership Model is expressed in as many unique ways as the individuals and/or organizations applying it.

When you combine the components (and their sub-elements) you can see that the distinctions – aspiration, integration, and caring – together create a very potent force for good. *And that would be you.* (Figure 2.5)

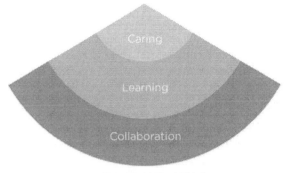

COMMUNITY

Figure 2.4

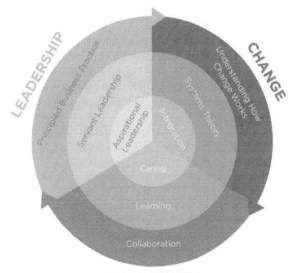

COMMUNITY

Figure 2.5

"What Does Emergent Leadership Look Like?"

As noted elsewhere, emergent leadership is expressed in as many ways as the individuals and/or organizations applying it – like a snowflake. To better grasp how the EMERGE Leadership Model might apply, it's helpful to look at real-life practitioners of emergent leadership.

David Eisenberg, co-founder of the <u>Development Center for Appropriate Technology (DCAT)</u> headquartered in Tucson, AZ, is a perfect example of emergent leadership and an original member of the EMERGE Faculty. For many years David has been quietly helping to correct the course taken by our system of building codes and the institutions that create, implement, and interpret them. And he does not simply say, "You are wrong, and here's what you have to do to be right!" He often shares this story:

Surprised by having only half the time I'd planned on for a presentation to about a thousand building code officials several years ago, I dropped my rehearsed conclusion. Instead, I asked a series of questions having to do with why anyone would want permission to build with alternative materials or methods. (Is it because they care about wanting to do the right thing?) And how, as a code official who also cared about doing the right thing, might one respond to this request? (Could you perhaps help them do it safely?) By their positive reaction (laughter, applause) it was clear I'd hit a chord. I quickly shut up and sat down. (David usually gets a few laughs at this point.)

Without really planning to, David had changed the conversation. He'd appealed to the hearts and minds of the code officials in attendance, opening the door to a continuing dialogue that has expanded the lens that code officials use, pointing beyond their very familiar and longstanding list of proscribed risks (e.g., fire, structural failure, and moisture) to the long-term upstream and downstream impacts – of toxic building materials, for example. Through DCAT and the larger community within which he works, David presents himself as a resource, rather than a critic, to code officials and their organizations, providing information and technical assistance. The result is two-fold: a better understanding of the unintended consequences that come from a limited view of the risks that we incur when we build, and the will to begin modifying codes to reflect the larger view. Now, many code officials are resources rather than barriers when someone approaches their counter with an innovative idea.

David's leadership style is one of service, and certainly aspirational, since he can only influence code development, not control it. He utilized some of the basic premises of change science when he helped code officials see the gap between the health and safety risks they were focused on and those lurking outside their field of view. By using education to show the benefits of addressing these risks – and the downside of ignoring them – and by bringing confidence to the feasibility of addressing these risks through pilot projects and compelling research, David has encouraged and also participated in the collaborative effort to develop the International Green Construction Code. Suffice it to say that he's a strong believer in the power of relationship! He's also encouraged community among code officials that are trying to do the right thing.

The irony is that David didn't choose to be a leader. He fell into the role by virtue of the fact that he wanted some answers for his personal practice, started asking questions, and created some energy around the idea that building codes could accommodate "alternative" methods...so much so that many of these methods are no longer considered so "alternative."

David continues to catalyze dialogue around the risks presented by conventional building practices, and he relishes opportunities to address them through changes in code construction and interpretation. David has recently turned his leaderly eye on the dangers of fire retardants in foam insulation.

Although practically speaking it is important that individuals wanting to provide effective leadership, whether emergent or not, have solid technical knowledge and some experience of the field in which they are hoping to lead, grey hair is not required. Brett Marlo DeSantis is a thirty-something mother of two young girls who runs her own design-build firm in Gig Harbor, Washington. Within three months of being exposed to emergent leadership principles during an intensive workshop and preparing her personal leadership plan, Brett had completed all three of her 90-day goals. (More about how you can do this in Chapter 14.)

Brett has continued to show leadership in her community through her participation in local non-profits, service clubs, and city boards such as the Downtown Waterfront Alliance, Rotary, Cascadia Green Building Council, and the Design Review Board for the City of Gig Harbor. She is vice-president of Harbor WildWatch, a marine and environmental education organization dedicated to inspiring stewardship for the Puget Sound. She writes green building columns for multiple publications and has recently started a social purpose corporation (S.P.C.) named *Aaah*, with a purpose and passion to transform the built environment by creating an affordable, adaptable alternative housing model that is healthy and sustainable for all. (More on social purpose corporations in Chapter 15.) Brett has also won several awards for best of design + customer service and is now Living Future Accredited and excited to begin her first Living Building Challenge project. *Go Brett!*

Emergent leadership is something to be explored and developed over a lifetime. But if you are dedicated to personal growth and honest about where you are in space and time you can start practicing it immediately. This makes the EMERGE Leadership Model especially invaluable in a time of urgency such as the present. We can't really wait until everyone's earned their societal "stripes" or managed to acquire their white steed to address the dearth of sustainability in our built environment and community policies.

3

If Emergent Leadership Is Aspirational, What Are We Hoping For?

As should be clear from this book's introduction, I have a not-so-hidden agenda. There are many excellent books and workshops promoting and informing effective leadership. This book and the EMERGE Leadership Project are not simply about offering a better way to be a successful leader per se. There is a "cause" attached, and that cause is the transformation of the built environment through the imagination and application of life-sustaining solutions.

It is also aspirational, and in that light, the "successful (emergent) leader" is committed to – *aspires to* – influencing a change in conditions for the social good. This commitment does not require emergent leaders to resign themselves to wearing sackcloth, seeking alms, and painting their faces with road dust. As noted earlier, more leaders are needed, and they need to be working more effectively in a multitude of locations, within a multitude of systems – from the largest corporations to the smallest organization. Any organizational entity that makes decisions that address how a built environment impacts resources now or in the future is an appropriate context for an emergent leader to work.

What does the sustainable transformation of the built environment look like? When we discuss the transformation of our built environment in the context of EMERGE, we are talking about deep, systemic change towards a sustainable reality.

Let's start with the word "sustainability." This ecologically-derived term has taken a beating, so right away let's make sure we are using the same understanding. The word's been co-opted, diluted, and made murky for marketing purposes that are sometimes admirable – and sometimes dubious. People frustrated with the marketing hash that's been made of the green building movement, and its incremental progress, have wrongly interpreted sustainability to mean "just good enough not to be bad." Some have even lobbied to introduce other terms to re-brand and further inspire the movement.

Yet *sustainability* is precisely what we are trying to achieve. Abandoning it would be like saying, "Gravity is so old hat. Let's find another term to describe how things fall to the ground that 'resonates'!"

You are probably most familiar with the definition of sustainability offered in an international economic development policy document published in 1987. According to the Brundtland Commission, originator of the document, sustainability is defined as "meeting the needs of the present without compromising the ability of future generations to meet their needs" (United Nations World Commission on Economic Development 1987, 41). This statement has been used to define the purpose of green building since the term "green building" was conceived in the early 1990s. That it actually came out of the economic development world, and was applied to much more than the environment, and certainly more than the built environment, gives us a clue as to the depth and breadth of the meaning of sustainability.

The (U.S.) National Commission on the Environment – a private sector initiative convened by the World Wildlife Fund – shed a little more light on the term when it asserted, "Sustainable development mandates that the present generation must not narrow the choices of future generations but...expand them by passing on an environment and an accumulation of resources that will allow its children to live at least as well as, and preferably better than, people today" (National Commission on the Environment 1993, 2). By including the concept of *expanding* choices, the NCOE introduced the idea that restoration is a part of sustainability, as well as the quality of life the future holds.

On his website, Dr. John R. Ehrenfeld, former Director of the MIT Program on Technology, Business, and the Environment, describes sustainability as "the possibility that humans and other life will *flourish* on Earth forever" (johnehrenfeld.com, post June 11, 2015, my italics).

Sustainability is not about simply surviving. It is about thriving. When an infant is provided food, clothing, shelter, but not hugged, what happens? It fails to thrive, and may even die. That's not sustainable.

In an article discussing the release of *Beyond the Limits to Growth* in 1992, authors Donella Meadows, Dennis Meadows, and Jorgen Randers stress that their first book, *Limits to Growth* (released in 1972), was not a prediction but a challenge: "to bring about a society that is materially sufficient, socially equitable, and ecologically sustainable, and one that is more satisfying in human terms..." (Meadows, et. al 1992, 2). While reinforcing that sustainability is about the environment, this statement makes clear that we are talking about much more.

Ehrenfeld also notes that "reducing unsustainability, although critical, will not create sustainability." That's because we are not talking about a mathematical equation. We *are* talking about balance, a *dynamic* balance. And as the policy makers and scientists have pointed out, we are talking about restoring this dynamic balance by addressing the issues in *all* living systems.

Restoring the Dynamic Balance of All Living Systems

SOCIAL • COMMERCIAL • NATURAL

Figure 3.1

In Figure 3.1, you can see I've defined "living systems" to include social, commercial, and natural systems. (You've probably heard of the three E's - equity, economy, or environment; or the three P's - planet, people, profit. It's the same thing, just without the alliterative punch.)

In the diagram there is an upward spiraling trend towards dynamic balance, with the goal to move

from a mindset of "doing less harm" to "doing some good." In the past, I've drawn this process as a rightward linear process. (I've also seen some renditions of the progression as upward, but still linear. While recognizing that we are speaking of an idealized process, the linear approach is not helpful. Spiral imagery makes more sense because, as green building practitioners and/or advocates, it often feels like we are just going around in circles, revisiting topics and outcomes. Yet the spiral encourages us. We *are* making progress. And an open spiral encourages us to view our work (and progress) from many perspectives, simultaneously. We can see where we've been and where we are going. We can communicate easily and openly with others on the spiral.

In the past we have struggled (and still do) with describing progress towards sustainability. Light, medium, and dark green, barely legal, legal, and beyond code, are just some of the labels we have used. Graphic illustrations have portrayed progress as a straight arrow traveling to somewhere specific. We've been treating sustainability as a destination, someplace static.

One proof that this "begin here, end there" approach doesn't really define our reality can be seen in the regulatory constraints related to building, and building green. The codes have often been used to separate the laggards from late majority and early adopters, acting as a bottom line. Ironically, when, as early adopters, we attempt to move the needle, we run smack into legal hurdles again. It's part of a progressive spiral - we've just "straightened" one of the loops! (See Figure 3.2, next page.)

Sustainability as a Destination

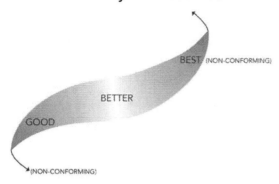

Figure 3.2

When we focus our resources (including most importantly our minds and hearts) on the restoration of a dynamic balance to "all" living systems, we are interacting with all sorts of systems – e.g., physical, social, political, economic, ecological – systems that overlap and interact in many ways from very well to very poorly.

So when I refer to sustainable transformation of the built environment, I am talking about more than brick and mortar and soil and landscaping and pervious parking lots. I'm talking about sustainability at this more comprehensive level.

In fact, one of the things that delighted me most about my work in green building was finding ways to tap into the larger opportunity for transformation through the practical (and seemingly mundane) decisions and processes we use to shape our built environment. Having this systems view of the overall "project" we call green building adds to the work's complexity. However, it also makes the effort much richer than it would be if we simply restrained ourselves to thinking about the process in terms of "trade-offs," checklists, and mandates. The emergent leader treats

the concept of spiral progression as a tool for this larger work. As you will see, the spiral will be used in multiple ways to both describe what we are working toward, and how we are working toward it.

I've been privileged to work in the Northwest for many years, where I have been part of many projects that were ostensibly about things like how much recycled content was included in the project, or how many points the project earned, or what threshold a project achieved. Certainly, these milestones were causes to celebrate, but for me, the excitement came when I saw changes in awareness and attitude toward the process of shaping (and re-shaping) our built environment, environmental stewardship, and greater understanding of the creativity those changes unleashed.

The practice of green building within the context of an explicit and genuine desire for sustainability can do so much good on so many levels. In addition to the conservation of resources through the life of the project, it can inspire new business models, create meaningful opportunities for work, instigate technological innovation, offer equity to the marginalized, be a source of civic pride, foster collaboration among diverse parties, and much more. I don't feel I'm exaggerating when I say that the practice of green building (again, within the proper context) can be a tool for positive human development.

The Bertschi School's "Living Building Science Wing" is one example of what I mean. It's highlighted in the first of several "Transformation in Practice" (TIP) case studies included in the book. The projects and initiatives described in the TIPs all promote green building, but they are also exemplars of the richness such projects can offer in terms of catalyzing "true" sustainability.

With every green building project, program, or policy, the emergent leader is ever on the lookout for transformational opportunities. As you review the examples throughout the book, imagine the ingredients in play that could explain success. Think about projects in which you have participated, and which you believe have been transformative "beyond brick and mortar." How did you personally foster transformation? What did you learn from your experiences that is transferable to other projects?

TRANSFORMATION IN PRACTICE:
The Bertschi School Living Building Science Wing

The Bertschi School, a private, non-profit primary school, possesses an environmental, community, and civic ethic that carries over to the design, construction, and operation of its campus buildings. The Bertschi School enrolls 235 students within a seven-building campus spanning half of a city block (shared with single family housing) in Seattle Capitol Hill neighborhood.

The Bertschi School's green building leadership was recognized in 2008 when the School's new gymnasium and community building earned LEED Gold certification. Features such as the living wall (see photo) in its Science Wing earned it the designation as one of the top ten green designs of 2013 by judges in AIA Seattle's juried "What Makes It Green?" competition. That same year, the school achieved Washington Green Schools certification, a program focused on green operations, well before others in the state (O'Brien, DeNamur, & O'Brien, 142).

The Science Wing eventually became the fourth project in the world and the first in Washington State to achieve full certification under the Living Building Challenge.

All laudable achievements. But for the purpose of this discussion, I want to focus on the unusual and exciting developments this transformative atmosphere fostered, none of which have to do with brick and mortar. The Bertschi School was not just choosing to make more sustainable buildings; they were choosing to share with the world what they did, how they did it, and the results of their efforts. The Living Building Challenge encourages and supports this transparency, with hope of transforming the built environment and the market that shapes it.

In the case of Bertschi, a group of Seattle-area designers and consultants, organized as the Restorative Collective, offered to work *Pro Bono* for the school because they wanted to gain experience with both the new Living

Building Challenge and with integrative design and to "construct an informed foundation for designing buildings to [meet] the 2030 Challenge and [create] net-zero buildings" (O'Brien August 1, 2013). Bertschi and the Collective signed a contract that "call(ed) out our intent to meet the Living Building Challenge and achieve Living Building Certification," according to Stan Richardson, the school's Director of Campus Planning (O'Brien et. al., 148) yet specified a design fee of zero. Besides the obvious, that design services are rarely (intentionally) contributed for free in today's tight economy, the group comprised members of firms that quite frequently competed with each other. Significantly, they undertook a transparent process among potential and actual competitors to learn together, certainly an approach in line with emergent leadership practice, and in a world where competition and trade secrets are prized over transparency. What's more, their intentional contribution inspired the contractor to do the work at cost and to negotiate with the subs to make similar financial sacrifices.

If you ask them, and I have, the individuals (owners, designers, builders) involved will tell you their contribution was worth it, in particular because of the practical lessons they learned in applying the Living Building Standard and trying on the integrated design process. (Note that none feel that they had achieved the ideal for either.) They continue to share the lessons they learned from this project at conferences, in articles, and through their firms' websites. Elizabeth Powers, Nicole DeNamur, and I were given full access when writing an article for the University of Washington Environmental Law & Policy Journal on the legal hurdles faced by those wanting to design, construct, and operate deep green buildings. (See References.) The article was another ripple in the transformative pond this project helped feed, this time reaching out into the legal community, hoping to influence land use planning and regulations, leasing instruments, and contract practices.

Also discussed in the article was the fact that the project resulted in manufacturers modifying products to be eligible for design specifications for the Living Building Challenge. Conversations with the design team resulted in CrystaLite, Inc. removing PVC from their skylight system, and Flotender™ removing PVC from their greywater treatment system.

A final note about the project: It clearly has had a transformative influence on those of us that design, build, operate, and regulate buildings (and make products for them). Perhaps more exciting though is the impact it had on the children who attend the school. Lined up on the sidewalk of the residential Seattle neighborhood where the school is located were sixth graders from the school celebrating the groundbreaking for the new Science Wing. They were chanting, "Living Building! Living Building! Living Building!" These kids were seriously interested and celebrating their grand, green school. They understood the importance of getting it right. I'm guessing they felt curious about what their lives would be like in the new building. I'm guessing too, they felt cared for because of the way they were included in the design of the project. (Students wanted to bring the "stream" of rooftop rainwater inside, as you can see in the photo.)

Photo(s) Credit: Benjamin Benschneider.

Links for more project information:

http://www.bertschi.org/who-we-are/our-campus/science-wing/

http://living-future.org/case-study/bertschiscience

Hellstern, Chris, 2014, Living Building Education: The Evolution of Bertschi School's Science Wing, Ecotone Publishing: Portland, OR

Back to Basics

The first component of the EMERGE Leadership Model provides the prospective emergent leader with a framework to explore your personal leadership practice – how you lead now and how you could lead for better results. As noted earlier, the Leadership component is made up of three tiers: principled business practice (the foundation), servant leadership (the centerpiece), and aspirational leadership (the distinction). (Figure 4.1)

Aspirational Leadership

Servant Leadership

Principled Business Practice

LEADERSHIP

Figure 4.1

Emergent leadership moves us away from conventional leadership practice, and that is a good thing. To borrow from Albert Einstein's oft-quoted declaration that "doing the same thing over and over again and expecting different results is a form of insanity," leading in the same way and expecting the kind of transformation we need to be truly sustainable is wishful thinking at best. If we want different results, we need to change the way we lead.

As noted earlier, emergent leadership is particularly useful for transformative work because it does not require charisma or power of position. As a result, more individuals can apply it at more places in the system(s) where change needs to happen. We have a systems problem, which we need to address strategically. Further, because of its emphasis on service, emergent leadership encourages us to let go of egotistical motivations, which helps us keep our eyes on the prize.

Emergent leaders understand how change works, and why people gravitate towards particular goals. They employ proven and practical psychology to create conditions favorable to change. I'm not talking about manipulation by a masterful leader. By treating every situation as a collaborative and potentially transformative one, by approaching these opportunities with curiosity, rather than anxiety, emergent leaders create positive relationships. We open the door to possibilities, we can better imagine solutions, and we achieve these solutions collectively.

In our society, people often think significant change happens only with large infusions of cash – money to fund interventions such as education, enabling policy work, incentives, disincentives, and so forth. These interventions are important, and yet they are futile without another resource that has nothing to do with money: *People.*

People make choices that represent change or business as usual, making *relationships* among people the most important resource for change. And with emergent leadership, we work toward creating *positive relationships.* We treat those we hope to

influence for change as partners in the change, partners in our shared future.

The foundational tier for the Leadership component is called, for lack of a better term, "principled business practice." This idea encompasses the large body of best practices found in the best business leadership and management literature and exemplified by forward-thinking business leaders such as James Sinegal. Founder and former CEO of Costco, Sinegal was known to foster meaningful relationships with his employees by "walking the floor" on a regular basis. Costco has been unique in the world of big-box retailers, providing health benefits to its employees without being forced to, for example.

Principled business practice is uncommon in the business world, but it is the minimum we would ask of an emergent leader. What does this level of leadership require? Study after study cited by respected business writers points to three traits that employees consistently desire in their managers, and which are exhibited by the most effective business leaders. A principled business leader is *ethical*, *open*, and *credible*.

As Figure 4.2 illustrates, each of these three traits is comprised of certain characteristics. An *ethical* business manager acts with integrity, is congruent between actions and statements, and is fair or just in those actions. An *open* business manager is attentive and consultative (that is, they communicate with those they are managing before making decisions that would impact them significantly). And a *credible* business manager is one who achieves what they set out to do most of the time and is accountable when

> ### Figure 4.2: What Research Tells Us We Want in a Principled Business Leader
>
> - Ethical
>   - Honest
>   - Congruent
>   - Fair
> - Open
>   - Attentive
>   - Consultative
> - Credible
>   - Effective
>   - Accountable
>
> *(Derived from multiple sources: but primarily Kouzes & Posner, 2007, 2003)*

they don't.

If these are the characteristics of a principled business leader, how does such a leader behave for best results? In *The Leadership Challenge*, one of the texts you will find in most progressive MBA curricula, authors Kouzes and Posner provide several steps one can take to meet the challenge of good leadership: *model the way*, *inspire*, *challenge*, *strengthen*, and finally, *encourage* on behalf of those they lead. (I studied *The Leadership Challenge* 4th edition in 2007. There is now a 25th Anniversary 5th Edition, which came out in 2012.)

Let's explore these steps and see how they might apply for a principled business leader working in the field of sustainability.

Model the Way: You've probably heard this expressed as "walking your talk." In conventional business management practice, the assumption is that a person in the role of manager is modeling the desired behavior. Inherent to emergent leadership – recall the concept of leading from any chair – is the assumption that no matter what position you hold, you can model the preferred path. As an emergent leader, you model sustainable leadership to your peers, your direct reports, and your supervisors through the decisions you make and *how* you make them. And you can inspire, challenge, and strengthen your organization and/or community's capacity to follow your example. When Costco embraced health care for its employees, it announced it to the world in an effort to inspire similar businesses to follow their example.

Inspire: Most managers stop after describing what will happen if no action is taken. However, a really good manager can describe the destination so imaginatively that the people they manage will volunteer for the trip. The assumption is that you have to be an entertainer to entice people to come along with you. But you can inspire others just by being yourself. *Tell your story.* When did you "get religion" – and how did it happen? Elicit stories from those you are leading.

Make your story personal. Early on in the development of construction & waste management and recycling practices for a major contracting firm, I learned from one-on-one conversations that site crew members most committed to the effort were those who'd gotten in trouble at home for throwing aluminum cans in the garbage. Their school-age kids were yelling at them! I encouraged them to share the experience at one of the weekly job-site meetings. It made for a good laugh, but it also illuminated the fact that, for some, environmental stewardship was something they could do for their kids. It made it personal. It also highlighted the accountability we all have towards the next generation – an important aspect of sustainability.

And make your story visual. It was probably entertaining when my colleagues and I climbed into a job-site waste container to conduct an audit on that same job site. (In fact, I know it was amusing because the site crew smirked as we dove into the stinky mess of discarded lunches and other garbage.) Later, we showed slides of what we had pulled out of the container – recyclables that had been tossed in with the garbage – and which we had neatly arranged into piles of cardboard, wood, metal. Those same crew members were understandably dismayed. Up to that point they had been proud of their recycling efforts, which were also touted in giant banners attached to the construction fence. We took the sting out of the audit results with baked cookies, because it wasn't about shaming them, but showing them. Disappointed in themselves, they focused their efforts, and the next audit was much improved.

Challenge: Back when the U.S. General Services Administration (GSA) was first looking at LEED and considering how it could apply to their projects, they hired me to consult on an in-progress federal project. As part of my contract, I attended a design team meeting where I listened to a discussion of what to do about the landscaping. The facility in question was located in a historically agricultural area, known especially for its orchards, so the site plan was calling for an orchard-like design to reflect the prior, historic use. The GSA project managers had learned though that the facility staff didn't like the idea of picking up after dropped fruit, so the discussion then revolved around planting trees that looked like apple trees

but had been bred to bear no fruit. In other words, fruitless! The irony was not lost on me. However, I simply asked, "What would the site look like if it hadn't been developed by humans?" They responded, "Sage and high desert vegetation." Then I asked, "Why not honor the natural origins of the site, especially if real apple trees are not an option?"

Sometimes, as leaders we need to challenge assumptions or simply ask: "Why would we do this?" In the above case, the project planners wanted to honor place and history – certainly a sustainable practice. But they lost their way, I think, when they started down the path to creating what felt to me like an agricultural theme park. I would love to report that this group simply raised their coffee cups in hosanna to my idea, but as with many projects in the early days, I had been brought in very late. I lacked the benefits of good timing and familiarity with the players, both of which would have been present if they'd been using an integrative process, and I'd been a part of that. (More on that later.)

Strengthen: This step to meet the challenge of good leadership means providing training, guidance, and "tools" – all with an eye to developing the capacity of the individual to do the work you are expecting them to do. With principled business practice, you don't leave people hanging out to dry. With emergent leadership, strength is about more than making your employees more capable; it's about building the capacity of your peers, clients, members of the community, and, dare I say it, your competitors! In presenting proposals to clients I would tell them, "If we finish the project and your organization doesn't have an increased capacity to make sustainable decisions and implement sustainable practice, then we haven't done our job." "parallel play."

Encourage: This step seems like a no-brainer. And yet how many times have you been in a position as an employer where you've forgotten that even the most productive self-starter still needs to be acknowledged for their work? You know the value of acknowledgement if *you* are that productive self-starter, don't you!? Encouragement means giving credit where it is due. It means highlighting positive behavior. It also means paying enough attention, and caring enough to gently correct when you see something that's below standard. You don't do anyone any favors when you ignore incompetency or mistakes, hoping they will correct themselves over time or even go away! With clients and colleagues, realistic encouragement can be just as important. For example, At O'Brien & Company, we instituted the Hummingbird Award for individuals who, like hummingbirds, were tenacious and enthusiastic in "pollenating" sustainable ideas within the company and our client community. The winner would be responsible for choosing the next winner, and would get to present the award at a staff meeting.

Mentoring

On a one-to-one basis, principled business leadership is best represented through the practice of mentoring. The five most commonly used mentoring techniques found in a classic on the subject, *Working Wisdom: Timeless Skills and Vanguard Strategies for Learning Organizations* (Aubrey and Cohen, 1995) include:

Accompanying: The mentor and the learner work side by side. There is no formal "teaching" or explicit information exchange taking place. You might call this

Sowing: This mentoring technique often occurs through questions (often provocative) or storytelling (usually of personal experience) and is generally performed by the mentor, with the understanding that the mentee may not be ready to change. As the term sowing implies, one is "planting the seed" for the change that is anticipated or hoped for when the situation requires it.

Catalyzing: The mentor chooses to plunge the learner right into change, provoking a different way of thinking. This is often called a "test by fire." The important thing here is for the mentor to understand the value of providing a "safety net" (just in case), or in some way be ready to deal with the consequences in a respectful manner.

Showing: As a mentor, you use your own example to demonstrate a skill or activity. The best demonstration is in alignment with information you have provided or exchanged through the other mentoring practices – known in common sense terms as "practicing what you preach." Don't require that every project meeting have a stated purpose but then improvise the meetings you lead!

Harvesting: The mentor focuses on "picking the ripe fruit" and helps the mentee become aware of what was learned by experience and to draw conclusions. The mentor can ask: "What have you learned?" and "How might you use this information?"

I have had the privilege of mentoring many individuals over the years, especially as President of

O'Brien & Company. When the company was small, this guidance would happen naturally as part of the day. It helped that we had a small office with an open plan. I was pretty accessible. My less experienced colleagues could hear me on the phone dealing with challenging issues. They could ask me advice about something they were dealing with at the moment. We could swap stories. We could arrange a quick cup of coffee when it seemed like we both needed a break.

As the company grew, however, we realized we needed to institutionalize some form of mentorship to make sure it didn't get lost in the everyday details of work. We designed an internal coaching system, pairing each staff member with a principal. After a certain amount of time, we'd rotate out so that staff members would get the benefit of working with all the principals in this manner. (We developed an agenda and guidelines for the coaching session. See bonus materials for this chapter for examples.) If this system is too onerous, which it could prove to be for small companies needing to keep overhead to a minimum, you can consider streamlining the meeting schedule to match professional development timelines. Regardless, it is always important for the mentor to take advantage of teachable moments - they may not happen on a "schedule."

During my tenure with O'Brien & Company, I was also blessed with requests from young professionals for informational interviews and coffee meetings to discuss professional aspirations. My favorite meetings were with students in the Sustainable Building Advisor program. They were smart and committed and dedicated to making a difference. It wasn't just a career for them, but *a calling* - which

is how I feel today when I mentor EMERGE alumni. These sessions are incredibly satisfying, as both the mentor and mentee take the relationship and the time commitment seriously.

To be a good mentor, it can help to have been a mentee. I'm a book-learner, so when I formed my sole proprietorship in 1991, I read many books about business management. I formed a fake "board" made up of friends with business and marketing skills, and once a year I'd send "my board" a draft annual report and plan for review. We'd get together over a meal to discuss their comments. I got excellent advice about setting fees (which I wished I'd followed better), managing employees vs. contracted staff, working with lenders. For a small business owner, it was ideal.

When it came to the "content" of my profession, however, there were few individuals who could play the role of mentor. We were all starting out! So I sought out colleagues whom I respected and - with their permission - used them as sounding boards. (And they looked to me for similar feedback, too.) We would talk by phone, usually long distance (when that mattered!), or at conferences, discussing existing projects and ideas for new work, including, often, ideas for collaboration. I still do this today with the EMERGE Leadership Project.

Over the years I have discovered that though most peers can provide encouragement, only some are good at providing constructive criticism. So with the big questions, I gravitate toward those who can be honest *and* loving - excellent attributes for a mentor.

Humility: The other quality I notice in the peers who

have mentored me best is humility. For them, it's not about their egos, it's about the relationship. This characteristic of humility leads us naturally to the next level of leadership, where prospective emergent leaders consider how an attitude of service can foster growth in themselves, as well as those we hope to lead.

Having an explicit mentoring arrangement can create a safe container for frank, and possibly difficult, conversations. There may be times, however, when you find yourself providing advice to a colleague on an impromptu basis on a matter about which you might have more experience. On such occasions, one's goal may be to make that which is implicit explicit, in order to avoid misunderstanding. Does your colleague want your advice? Or did they simply need you to listen?

TRANSFORMATION IN PRACTICE:
South Lake Union (SLU) District

In the early 90s, the SLU neighborhood located in downtown Seattle was a sparsely populated area that included some industrial manufacturing businesses, some low- rent art housing, derelict buildings, and lots of paved surface parking lots. At that time, a citizen initiative to create a central park failed. However, another initiative to redevelop the area (indicated by shading in the aerial photo) with the idea of creating more density, more jobs, and more vitality in the area took its place.

There was private and public sector interest in understanding how the area could be developed sustainably. The Urban Environmental Institute, along with a multi-disciplinary consultant team sponsored by Vulcan, Inc. and led by Mithun, studied how speculative development could employ economically viable sustainable practices that create value using South Lake Union as a case study. According to the study's executive summary, the team was challenged to "develop recommendations that would be 'repeatable' within the larger development community" (Urban Environmental Institute 2002, 6). Thus it was true from the beginning that the South Lake Union District was intended by forward thinkers to be a transformative model for other urban development. (For the original document, see references.) The results of the study were encouraging enough to support enabling public policy, which in turn led to private investment and many green building "firsts" – including the first LEED apartment building in Seattle, the first LEED laboratory in the U.S., and the first spec LEED building in the city.

As of this writing, there are more LEED buildings open or under way in South Lake Union than anywhere else in Seattle. Between green building and transportation projects, such as vehicle recharging stations, Seattle's first modern electric streetcar, and a "green street" project, the SLU District has come a long way toward its goal to re-invent itself (See photo). But if new green buildings and infrastructure were all that resulted, it would not have achieved the larger public/private vision of a vital, thriving neighborhood. The District's grocery stores, retail businesses, and new streetcar line serve a population that is growing – at ten times the rate of growth in other Seattle neighborhoods. The density sought is happening. The apartments and condos serve many singles, and many families, too. Household growth in SLU significantly outpaces other neighborhoods in Seattle – so much so that there is discussion about building a new public elementary school in the neighborhood. Amazon offices and bio-tech firms in the District have confirmed that the job growth hoped for was not a pipe dream.

Despite the 2008 recession, net job growth in South Lake Union has been substantial, even when considering losses due to businesses that have been replaced. And the design community and City of Seattle have continued to refine the overall vision for the neighborhood, developing guidance for implementation in The South Lake Union Urban Design Framework (City of Seattle + Weber Thompson 2010).

Illustration used with permission of Vulcan.
Photo credit: Benjamin Benschneider
Links for more information:
http://www.discoverslu.com/slu-discovery-center/
http://en.wikipedia.org/wiki/South_Lake_Union,_Seattle
http://www.seattle.gov/dpd/cityplanning/completeprojectslist/southlakeunion/whatwhy/

How Can I Serve?

The centerpiece for the Leadership component of the EMERGE Leadership Model is *servant leadership* (Figure 5.1). To a certain extent, this is where my personal exploration of leadership began. In the mid-nineties – a few years after I started O'Brien & Company – a colleague used the phrase "servant leadership" in a conversation about business management. Without knowing much about the philosophy behind the concept, these words themselves resonated for me in a deeply profound way. I sensed a good "fit" between the terminology and my personal spiritual experience.

Figure 5.1

My Story

A cradle Catholic, I was generally more excited about the aspects of the faith tradition that focused on social justice than on saying my prayers. At a young age, I was drawn to the work of social activist and Catholic convert Dorothy Day – and later, further energized by the examples of civil rights leader Martin Luther King, Jr., and our first Catholic President,

John F. Kennedy. I felt JFK had asked me personally, "What can *you* do for your country?" As an adult, my spirituality took on a more eclectic feel, but the idea of making a difference to society was still prominent in my thinking, hopes, and activities – outside of work, at least.

It wasn't clear to me how my work meshed with this desire to serve personally. I understood that the content of my work was contributory. I knew intellectually that the environmental stewardship and economic development represented by green building was a good thing. And I understood that, as a business owner and employer, I was contributing to my community. But I wasn't experiencing this growing awareness as "service." That is, not until I had a personal "awakening" that connected the desire to serve with my work in a very practical way.

Years before my exposure to the term "servant leadership," I had the opportunity to propose on a project in a progressive city in northern Colorado. When I was shortlisted and asked to come for an interview, I was excited. However, as the owner of a small company with modest resources, the last-minute trip represented a huge investment. As the plane took off, I experienced tremendous misgivings about the entire matter. What was I doing spending $1,000 I didn't have? The scope in the RFP was ambiguous and rife with opportunities for "creep," and the budget was insufficient. Handling this project with my limited resources from Seattle seemed like a disaster waiting to happen. I leaned my head against the plane window and felt myself succumbing to a very dark mood. The closer I got to Colorado, the more depressed I felt. I wasn't sure how I'd gotten

myself into this mess. I worried. Should I be the one doing this work for them? Were the flaws in the RFP fatal? Did I even want the job? A thought came to me: *What if I told my prospective clients the truth?* It was one of those "light bulb" moments, and I felt my spirits lift. All was right with the world. The interview became less an interview and more a meeting to discuss what turned out to be mutual concerns. I didn't get the job, but I did feel useful. Apparently that mattered more to me. A year later, I received a call from the project manager, who shared that many of my fears about the project had been realized. I'm not sorry I didn't get that job, but the experience affirmed my belief that to be of service would always be more rewarding to me than making a lot of money (although that's nice too).

So, years later when my colleague shared the term "servant leadership" with me, the concept found fertile ground. At the same time, the idea that service could be linked with leadership (or even a form of leadership) was a completely new idea. I began to study the literature that was available on the subject and think about how to infuse the concept more explicitly into company philosophy. I assigned books to employees, such as Kent Keith's *Case for Servant Leadership* and Sipe and Frick's *Seven Pillars of Servant Leadership*, and we discussed the readings at company retreats.

Meanwhile, I earned a graduate certificate on the topic, during which time I learned the origins of servant leadership philosophy. The term "servant-leader" was coined in 1969 in an essay by Robert K. Greenleaf, after he had read Herman Hesse's *Journey to the East*. He interpreted the story's thesis as: "the great leader is seen as servant first, and that simple fact is the key to his greatness" (Greenleaf 2002, 21). Greenleaf, who was a Quaker, was a management consultant to AT&T and, later, a free-lance consultant on organizational leadership. He never defined "servant leadership," itself, but in that early essay, he described the "best test" of the idea: *"Do those served grow as persons, do they grow while being served, become healthier, wiser, freer, more autonomous, more likely themselves to become servants?"* (Greenleaf 2002, 27).

Servant Leadership

Scholars have expanded on Greenleaf's writings, which tend to be abstract. (Greenleaf himself admits to being challenged in presenting a logical argument for pursuing this form of leadership, as it "came to (him) as an intuitive insight" (Greenleaf 2002, 26). In *Seven Pillars of Servant Leadership*, Sipe and Frick define a "Servant-Leader as a *person of character* who *puts people first*. He or she is a *skilled communicator*, a *compassionate collaborator* who has *foresight*, is a *systems thinker*, and leads with *moral authority* (Sipe and Frick, 2009, 4). This definition is helpful in putting flesh on the bones of the concept, but it's important to never let go of Greenleaf's "best test" of servant leadership. It is what distinguishes "Servant Leadership" from "Principled Business Practice" – and it is certainly where the moral authority to lead is earned.

The motivation for a Servant-Leader is also a distinguishing factor. Greenleaf wrote, *"The first and most important choice a leader makes is the choice to serve, without which one's capacity to lead is severely limited."* Greenleaf alludes to the line that we in the sustainability field have drawn in the sand, the intention to "do no harm." He asks his readers to

be aware of the effect (of our leaderly actions) on the least privileged in society. He asks us to ask ourselves: "Will they benefit, or, at least, not be further deprived?" (Greenleaf 2002, 27).

Several of the definitive traits outlined by Sipe and Frick for a Servant-Leader are fairly straightforward and/or amply covered elsewhere. (Your favorite book outlet is rife with resources available to those interested in learning the "whys and wherefores" of communication and collaboration, for example. A few of my favorites on these and other topics are listed with other bonus materials under GOOD READS; see Author's Final Note.) One trait, however, stands out as the least transparent of those listed, yet I believe it is absolutely indispensable to the prospective emergent leader who aspires to lead for positive change. And that is *foresight*.

Foresight

Greenleaf described foresight as the only "lead" leaders have. "Without it, they are leaders in name only. They are not leading but are reacting to immediate events" (Greenleaf 2002, 40).

Larry Spears, servant leadership scholar, asserts that foresight is "hard to define, but easy to identify. One knows it when one sees it." He defines it as the ability to "understand the lessons from the past, the realities of the present, and the likely consequence of a decision for the future. It is deeply rooted in the intuitive mind." Spears goes as far as saying that foresight is "the one servant- leader characteristic with which one may be born" (Spears 1995, 6).

One might infer from Spears that some may be born

without foresight – which may be true, but I think unusual, since our survival as a species has depended on this ability to predict whether a situation is dangerous or not. One might also infer that there may be little you can do to develop it – and this I know is not true. Foresight is a kind of awareness, and there are ways to develop your capacity to be aware. Later we shall discuss some "awareness" practices and how they might be particularly helpful when discerning solutions for complex problems.

Practicing foresight at the level Greenleaf requires for a Servant-Leader does mean you have to live a "sort of schizoid life" where "one is always at two levels of consciousness. One is in the real world – concerned, responsible, effective, value oriented. One is also detached, riding above it, seeing today's events, and seeing oneself deeply involved in today's events in the perspective of a long sweep of history and projected into the...future." This split, says Greenleaf, allows "one better to foresee the unforeseeable" (Greenleaf 2002, 40).

But on a day-to-day basis how do you practice foresight? By combining logical thought processes with intuitive ones. Sipe and Frick outline five steps (Sipe and Frick 2009, 113-144):

1. Review the past
2. Learn everything there is to know about the issue
3. Let the information incubate
4. Be open for breakthroughs
5. Run your insights by others

When presenting this list at workshops, I get a lot of pushback on Step 2. Logically, we don't have time to learn *everything* there is to know before we need to take some action. As *managers*, we might want to control outcomes by covering all three bases, home plate, and the neighborhood outside the ball park. Obviously, we need to have a foundation for our approach to our work. But as leaders we use our intuition to balance our desire to control. Tapping into our intuition will help us know when we've learned enough for a particular situation. And we can trust that the information we need might come through indirectly working the *other* steps.

For each step, logic is balanced by intuition. For example, when you run your insights by others, logic tells you if what you are hearing back makes sense, while intuition helps you identify the "right" others to share your plans with. Both logic and intuition help you discern what's helpful about the feedback you are getting.

Foresight can often be making the best of a bad situation. In the sustainability field, we would call this *adaptation*. For emergent leaders seeking regenerative design solutions or restorative justice, we will want to proactively employ foresight. Sipe and Frick's five steps suggest you can practice foresight in non-emergency situations, and gain proficiency doing so. It will become second nature.

In the glossary for *Theory U*, American economist Otto Scharmer defines leadership as "the capacity of a system to sense and shape its future." He believes "the root of the word 'leadership' -- leith, [which] means 'to go forth,' 'to cross a threshold,' or 'to die' ...suggests that the experience of letting go and...

going forth into another world [which] begins to take shape only once we overcome the fear of stepping into the unknown, *is at the very heart and essence of leadership.*"(Scharmer, 2009, 467, my emphasis).

Applying Scharmer's understanding of leadership to the quality of foresight emphasizes the need for emergent leaders to use the past as information rather than prediction. There are often many "right" answers. It is tempting to land on the first "right" answer and then act. But taking a "foresightful" approach, and staying present to it as Scharmer suggests, will generate transformative solutions and help you discern the highest future possibility. Scharmer recommends we "explore the future by 'doing'." Rather than making a decision for all time, Scharmer suggests quickly developing a prototype based on your vision and/or intention, "something small, speedy, and spontaneous [that] quickly generates feedback" from the system and provides information that helps you evolve the idea" (Scharmer and Kaufer 2013, 21).

Pilot projects, when understood as experimental (that is, a next iteration is envisioned and provisionally funded) can be a practical application of foresight in action.

In addition to foresight, Sipe and Frick include the term "systems thinker" in their definition of a servant leader. We will discuss systems thinking later as part of our exploration of the second component of the EMERGE Leadership Model, *Change.* For now, understanding how a systems thinker thinks is pertinent to this discussion because it might help you evaluate your personal leadership practice.

The best source I know of for information about systems-thinking is *Thinking in Systems: A Primer* by Donella Meadows. The book was published posthumously in (2008) and contains the author's guidance on how to develop the systems-thinking skills she suggested were critical to address what she viewed were system failures: environmental degradation, war, poverty, hunger. Although I will draw on this invaluable source for a later discussion of strategic intervention in the context of the Model's Change component, I strongly encourage you to read the book yourself. In addition to a very accessible discussion of the mechanics of systems-thinking, Meadows' personal philosophy and humility provide a wonderful example of leaderly-thinking in general.

For a list of systems-thinker attributes, however, I've drawn from Dennis Meadows and Linda Booth Sweeney's book, *The Systems Thinking Playbook*, also a good read for the emergent leader. (See next page)

Many of these attributes require a dedication to something bigger than oneself, which is a perfect segue to discussion of the next tier in the Leadership component: Aspirational Leadership.

Figure 5.2: Attributes of a System Thinker

- Pays attention to and gives voice to the long term
- Considers the whole picture
- Changes perspective to see new leverage points in complex systems
- Looks for interdependencies
- Uses peripheral vision to see complex cause and effect relationships
- Anticipates consequences; identifies when unanticipated consequences emerge
- Understands how mental models create our futures
- Makes systems visible through mapping and models
- Studies resource flows (quantities/time) to identify disconnects
- Focuses on structure, not on blame
- Holds the tension of paradox and controversy without trying to resolve it quickly
- Watches out for "win/lose" mindsets
- Sees one as part of, not outside of, a given system

(Meadows and Sweeney 1995, 2)

TRANSFORMATION IN PRACTICE:
Rainier Beach Urban Farm and Wetlands Project

Rainier Beach Urban Farm and Wetlands (RBUFW) are located in southeast Seattle on a site previously occupied by the Atlantic City Nursery. The nursery was operated by Seattle Parks and Recreation for over 70 years, until early 2010 when it was closed for fiscal reasons. The nursery was reopened as RBUFW and is now run by Seattle Tilth and the Friends of RBUFW though the land is still owned by the Parks Department. The landscape architecture firm Berger Partnership was hired to develop a site master plan (see illustration), the focus of which was to apply innovative green infrastructure practices for the farm and wetland restoration while supporting experiential learning on multiple levels. The project qualifies as transformative in a number of ways: 1) by highlighting a policy barrier and providing the impetus to remove it; 2) by demonstrating ways to build community using a community's own resources; 3) by inspiring servant leadership; and 4) by offering significant potential for addressing the community's lack of food security.

Located in the heart of one of the nation's most diverse zip codes, the ten-acre site has the potential to produce over 20,000 pounds of fresh, healthy food each year for families in the Rainier Beach community, many of whom struggle with food security.

Unfortunately, despite the fact that the City of Seattle introduced progressive Urban Farming Codes in 2010, every one of the existing greenhouses on the property exceeds the maximum square footage the City allows for structures related to urban and in-ground farming. As a result the project needed to go before the Seattle City Council for approval. "While Seattle's municipal code approves urban agriculture as a land use, RBUFW highlighted some code challenges that needed to be addressed if urban agriculture is to get beyond P-Patches," says Rachael Meyer, project manager at Berger Partnership. The City Council did ultimately approve the project, providing a needed precedent for other urban farming efforts in residential zones.

The Berger Partnership approached O'Brien & Company early in 2012 to be a part of the design team. Rachael Meyer had attended the EMERGE Leadership Workshop and wanted help infusing the lessons of the EMERGE Leadership Model into the firm's plan for the project's collaborative design process. (The workshop team's whiteboard discussion resulted in the schematic for "emergent collaboration" that appears in Chapter 11.)

As anyone involved in community-based projects knows, the level of community engagement can range wildly. In the case of RBUFW, Berger Partnership was asked to facilitate an outreach process in which there was plenty of potential for community participation. In addition to Seattle Tilth and Friends of RBUFW, there were at least seven highly organized cultural groups organized around farming or cooking invested in what happens with the farm.

With this project, it was a matter of designing an outreach process that made good use of the already existing significant community interest. Ideally, the process would help identify both common and diverse interests, and result in an achievable plan that respects those interests and provides a foundation for long term and sustainable redevelopment of the farm.

Meyer notes, "It was really important for us [the firm] to avoid 'driving' the design agenda. In some ways the process was more important than a particular outcome. We needed to balance listening with designing." For RBUFW, the framework we white-boarded served as a tool to help the project team think about the process and understand its role. "Both the planning process and the resulting plan needed to be flexible, to allow for evolution over time." (Meyer, personal communication, 2013).

The potential for emergent leadership was already clearly in play with RBUFW. The key to success was to recognize this leadership component and structure the planning process to create a master plan that would nurture the relationships that would support the project going forward – long past the departure of the outside consultants. Meyer notes, "We had many meetings with different groups and different combinations of groups" and "wanted all of the stakeholders to hear and learn from each other." Seattle Tilth and the Friends of RBUFW supported this collaborative learning process, bringing in a demonstration food market stand during a meeting, and inviting local restaurants to cook and serve meals. These and other activities creatively drew connections between what was already happening in the community to what could be happening, without prescribing it.

The project's collaborative meetings highlighted the strong connection between eating together and community building. These meetings also helped spark one 9th grader's initiative linking gardening with friendship. This young woman, who attended the high school across the street, started a gardening club to grow food on the school campus, specifically to create a "better space to hang out with friends" (Meyer, personal communication, 2013). She asked Seattle Tilth (also involved in the school's culinary program) for help with the school garden, and quickly impressed everyone with her confidence despite her lack of experience. She was able to enlist schoolmates to participate in school work parties to create the garden she'd envisioned, and clearly she emerged as a leader in the process.

Presently, with the City Council's approval, the project can move beyond the planning phase. There has been a large-scale fundraising campaign involving the Seattle Parks Foundation, as well as securing grants from the State. Meyer notes the "team is working to bid the project and start construction so that farm improvements are completed in 2016" (Meyer, personal communication, July 2015).

Project illustrations courtesy of Berger Partnership.

Links for more information:

http://www.bergerpartnership.com/rainier-beach-urban-farm-and-wetlands/?id=category

http://www.seattle.gov/parks/projects/atlantic_city/nursery.htm

http://www.seattletilth.org/about/rainier-beach-urban-farm-wetlands

Leading For Positive Change

Aspiration distinguishes emergent leadership from servant leadership, in that we are leading with the goal of not simply growing those we lead for their own benefit, but also to catalyze a positive transformation in society. Since we don't have any control on society as a whole, we work strategically by leveraging our influence in societal systems.

Figure 6.1

Aspirational leadership, the "distinction" in the Leadership component of the EMERGE Leadership Model, (Figure 6.1) requires that our vision and value statements are congruent. Congruence between action and values and vision eliminates dissonance in the (energetic) field or space we are acting within, making positive change more likely. Says Margaret Wheatley, in her seminal work, *Leadership and the New Science*: "To learn what's in a field, look at what people are doing" (Wheatley, 2006, 55). For those of us hoping to lead, Wheatley suggests "We…be out there stating, clarifying, reflecting, modeling, filling" the field with the messages we care about (Wheatley, 2006, 57).

So we need to be clear about what our message is. Not just so we can communicate it to others in explicit ways, such as words and pictures, but so we can communicate it implicitly through our actions and the actions we support. As emergent leaders we need to be crystal clear about the vision and values we are aspiring to in the first place. We also need to fill the field we work in with "messages" that are congruent with that vision and those values.

Earlier in this book, I shared my hope that emergent leadership will bring about the transformation of the built environment, which will in turn result in a restoration of the sustainable balance of all living systems: natural, social, and commercial. I admit, this hope is a bit audacious. For the transformation of the built environment and a subsequent sustainable balance of all living systems to occur, it is imperative for each of you to determine how this super-sized vision translates to your daily emergent leadership practice. And that's what I'm asking.

What do you want to focus your leadership work on? What is your vision? What are the values underlying this vision? Many people assume that it is only organizations that need to do visioning work, but as an emergent leader you too need to create your own vision statement and understand your values. Any plan you create should be founded on your personal vision and values statement. Otherwise, you'll be focused on solving near-term problems without knowing if the results will be congruent with your vision and values. At a societal scale, this kind of "leadership" (really a lack thereof) is a form of "organized irresponsibility," according to Otto Scharmer and Katrin Kaufer. In their book *Leading from the Emerging Future*, the authors bemoan the fact that this leadership gap is "*collectively creating results that nobody wants*" (Scharmer and Kaufer 2013, 1, authors' italics).

In Chapter 14 we will focus on the practical work of creating a personal leadership plan, including tips for developing a vision and values statement. This chapter includes a discussion of the significance of personal growth for those aspiring to be agents of change. Let me share two skill-building disciplines that were significant to my personal growth and organizational work, and which I believe will be key competencies for prospective emergent leaders: *witnessing* and *acting "as if."*

According to Otto Scharmer, "We cannot transform the behavior of systems unless we transform the quality of attention that people apply to their actions within those systems, both individually and collectively" (Scharmer and Kaufer 2013, 19). There is great wisdom in this statement. And because I have experienced how witnessing has dramatically transformed the quality of my attention (and my behavior as a result) I believe the ability to "witness" is required for emergent leadership.

Witnessing is observing and articulating "what is" or "what has occurred" without judgment or blame. I liken it to doing an inventory in a grocery store. You wouldn't look at a dented can and scold it saying, "Bad can!" or an out-of-date jar and say, "Bad jar." Of course not! You'd just make a note: dented can, out of date jar. You wouldn't make a value judgment about the jar, because it is simply a jar that has expired. This attitude allows spaciousness around what the next indicated step might be.

I have used this skill-building tool of witnessing to inform my personal growth, to figure out why an interaction with an employee, client, friend, or a promising project went sideways, and to help jump-start organizational visioning sessions. It provides good information, and is a much easier way to get people with differing agendas to find common ground – even if the result is an agreed-upon observation, such as: "Some people feel THIS way, and some people feel THAT way!" It's just a fact that we can witness together, and be present to. (I liken it to sitting on the same side of the table, rather than across the table – it's a great visual that helps when things get a little rough.)

Witnessing provides a refreshing "breather" before the action starts. A useful tactic for personal interactions, it's also very helpful in group situations. To learn how to witness in group situations, I had to practice on myself first, performing a personal inventory when things felt "off." I do a daily check-in, whether I'm feeling stressed or not, so it is now (nearly) second nature to pull back when things are not going so well. I'll revisit the practice of witnessing again, in Chapter 11, when we discuss collaboration.

In addition to witnessing things that have happened or are happening, this practice can help us refrain from drawing too hard and fast conclusions about what "could" be – even when in our minds we are pretty sure the idea we have is a "good" one. Given our significant aspirations, we emergent leaders need to allow ourselves to stumble, if not gracefully, than graciously. It is possible to stay positive, even in the face of "failure." If we maintain our vision and values firmly in place, allowing them to act as our rudder, the tacks we need to take along the way are simply *tacks*

along the way – opportunities to learn.

It may be useful here to discuss "optimism." There are those, like myself, who default to "half-empty" glass thinking, and those who naturally default to "half-full" glass thinking. For both types, our job is to balance this tendency. In a website article summarizing Dr. Martin Seligman's views on flexible optimism, we learn why this balance is so important. "Optimism is good for us (but) on its own...can prevent us from seeing reality with clarity. It can help some people evade responsibility for their own failures; [and] it may work better in some cultures." Seligman, often called the "Father of Positive Psychology," suggests using "pessimism to achieve clarity when really big decisions have to be made" (Positive Psychology Resources, June 30, 2015).

Emergent leaders need to be resilient. They need to be able to move forward in the face of failure. Doing so assumes a level of humility, a quality often misunderstood as feeling "less than," when actually it's about feeling "right-sized." Not more than, not less than. Resilience frees you up to learn from each situation, and remain positive. But trying to *be* humble is nearly impossible. Whether naturally optimistic or pessimistic, the ego will get in the way. Practicing non-partisan witnessing, however, will generate the capacity to act with humility and think with flexible optimism.

One of the best ways I know to grow into a competency is to act "as if" I am already competent. I do my homework, of course, but the psychological benefit of "trying on" a behavior is huge. If I want to be a non-partisan observer, I have to consider that I can be one.

And if I fail at it, I can neutrally observe the failure and learn from it! You can't simply *think* you will behave in a new way. We humans just don't work like that.

Behaving like you are an emergent leader, one with aspirations of huge audacious goals, will help you become just such an emergent leader.

Constructive Facilitation

Constructive facilitation is a competency that is key to the success of collaborations, especially those you hope will be transformative. With constructive facilitation you have permission – and you must get permission! – to *question, synthesize,* and *contribute* information. This manner of facilitation goes beyond making sure everyone is heard. It is more directive and takes some courage. Your questions should provoke critical thinking or mindshifting – not defensiveness. That's a fine line. Your syntheses should be as inclusive as possible, and your contributions as positive as possible. In addition, when you take a "leaderly" stance, you need to be open to correction yourself. Perhaps you've missed a key point in the synthesis.

Constructive facilitation is a function of the maturation of the skills we've discussed thus far: the ability to apply foresight, with a combination of logic and intuition; the ability to witness, observe without bias, and to elicit witnessing behavior from the group you are facilitating; and acting "as if." The latter is important, since you must practice *acting "as if"* with others before this skill is fully baked. You'll make mistakes, and you will make them in public. In the early days of my career, I avoided too many bloopers by "partnering up" with a co-facilitator. We took turns taking the lead, which afforded each of us some space to witness what was happening, a break from the action, and more time to synthesize the facts and intuitive sensations swirling in the room.

As an emergent leader, your aim is to create a space where others can grow and be their best contributing selves for the best possible results. When you accept the role of constructive facilitator, your goal is to be seen not as a threat, but an asset.

To be perceived, and ideally accepted, as a skilled constructive facilitator, you must be as knowledgeable as possible about the group you are facilitating, with a sense of cultural attitudes, individuals who may act as leverage points and/or potential obstructions, historical desires, etc. This knowledge is what I call "discovery" and is the first important step in emergent collaboration, which is discussed further in Chapter 11.

TRANSFORMATION IN PRACTICE:
The Bullitt Center

Touted in the media as "the greenest commercial building in the world," the Bullitt Center (shown in photo) earned its Living Building certification on April 1, 2015. And it may well be, for the building has far surpassed its energy goal to be net zero energy, producing 60% more energy than it used in 2014 according to Brad Kahn with Groundwork Strategies (Kahn July 2, 2015). But its success achieving environmental goals is just a part of the story.

The Center is an exquisite example of how the built environment can act as a vehicle for change. Looking at the building, now 100% leased, it is easy to imagine the project's planners sitting around a table asking such questions as:

- "Can this building be a billboard for the living building challenge?"
- "Can it be a power plant?"
- "Can it pilot new policy?"
- "Can we break the law to raise the bar?"
- "Can we redefine commercial leasing with the planet in mind?"

In articles and presentations leading up to the project, it was clear that the Bullitt Foundation wanted to plan a transformative role in stimulating policy and market shifts that would accelerate adoption of the Living Building Challenge in the marketplace. Denis Hayes, President and CEO of the Bullitt Foundation, said, "If this building is alone five years from now this whole thing would have been a waste" (Bullitt Center, June 11, 2013). He and his group wanted to use the project experience and process to both create change and to highlight needed changes in codes and regulations that stand in the way of the innovation that the Living Building Challenge represents. Hayes points out correctly that, "If you really want to build a green building today in any city you'll find yourself in violation of maybe two dozen regulations and laws. The Bullitt Foundation wants to turn things on their head. They want the environmentally *sound* thing to be the *convenient* thing" (Bullitt Center, June 11, 2013).

And I think they're on the right track. Because of this project, there is now a Living Building Ordinance in the City of Seattle that provides some latitude in project planning in exchange for lessons learned. Because of this project, the "skybridge ordinance" was reviewed as a possible means to allow for the use of the airspace above the City's sidewalk for a PV installation. It was cost- prohibitive, but a workaround revealed itself. The PV installation was interpreted as an awning, so the cost was considerably less. (Kahn July 2, 2015).

Also, because of this project, the compost produced by its 20 composting toilets will be accepted at the local county's composting facility, merged with the county's product for distribution, and used to amend soil in the area. Because of this project, there is now clarification on the red tape standing in the way of a building's being self-sufficient water-wise – too much for most building owners. And, finally, because of this project, work is being done to smooth the way for more projects to achieve net-zero water. Like the Bertschi project, the Bullitt Center was used as a case study for addressing legal hurdles faced by deep green, high performing buildings in the article for the University of Washington's Environmental Law & Policy Journal mentioned previously. (See references.)

The Bullitt Center project has gained remarkable prominence in the marketplace. It's earned tremendous press because of the fact that it was designed and is being leased as commercial Class A space (see photo). As you might expect, the tenants include several organizations involved in the project, such as the International Living Future Institute, and the engineering firm, PAE Consulting Engineers.

The space is gorgeous and convenient, and being in the "greenest commercial building in the world" does lend a certain cachet. In a conversation with the leasing agent for the above mentioned article, In a telephone interview for the UW Law article, managing broker Angela Faul shared that the goal is "to provide the same opportunity to do business as successfully as in any great commercial Class A space" (Faul, June 5, 2013).

And then there's composting toilets no less! Before this project, compost toilet manufacturers had *no* experience producing a product that would meet the tolerances and dimensions for commercial Class A property. Because of this project they do now. A product that combines a flush toilet with composting toilet technology was developed to meet this project's specifications. Not only has the Bullitt Center project instigated product innovation, it has stimulated job creation.

Another success: The building wrap initially specified for the project included phthalates - "red list" material banned in the Living Building Standard. When questioned about the need to include phthalates, the manufacturer stated that the chemicals were integral to product performance. The project team said they weren't going to use it. What happened then? The manufacturer reformulated the product, tested it, and asked for re-consideration. In the end, this new wrap was installed on the project. Now this product – produced by Prosoco – is being specified on several green building projects in the Seattle area. As a result of making their product more planet-friendly, the manufacturer has opened the door to new business. This story also points out the transformative power of the Living Building Standard (when implemented by forward-thinking clients) to create greater product transparency, with the goal to influence product manufacturing for the good.

Photo Credits: Nic LeHoux
For more information:
http://www.bullittcenter.org/
http://living-future.org/bullitt-center-0

Understanding the Conditions for Change

As with the Leadership component, the Change component of the EMERGE Leadership Model includes three elements: a foundational tier, *Understanding How Change Works*; a centerpiece, *Systems Theory*; and the distinction, *Integration*. (Figure 7.1)

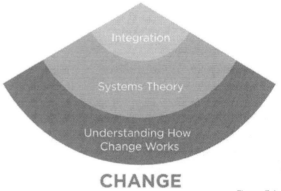

CHANGE

Figure 7.1

Emergent leadership requires us to think differently about how we approach change in others and ourselves. By understanding how change occurs, we can more effectively provide leadership with intention. At the same time, we accept the fact that we can't predict exactly what the change will look like. This unpredictability is a good thing, however, since there may be better possibilities out there. Our job is to foster the emergence of possibilities, without getting tied up in owning solutions, thereby placing us in a better position to lead toward results that are fitting, and therefore more likely to "stick."

A large body of behavioral science has shown there are conditions necessary for change to occur. As a prospective emergent leader you can learn to recognize where those conditions exist and how to leverage them. You can also learn to identify when those conditions are lacking and how to work to foster them.

This chapter explores both the factors researchers have identified as necessary for change to occur and the attitudinal spectrum along which individuals typically experience a "change process." I'll also discuss what science is telling us about which mechanisms for change work best, depending on where an individual is on that spectrum.

Conditions for Change

Much of the data on why and how people change their behavior comes from the health sector. Researchers in the field have been tasked with identifying how to improve overall health in the long term. Psychology professor, behavioral scientist, and author of *Changing For Good* (2007), James Prochaska in particular has conducted research and analysis that bears on the subject of conditions and mechanisms for change, some of the findings of which are now being used to inform social change projects. Along with colleagues John Norcross and Carlo DiClemente, Prochaska started by looking at successful self-changers – people who have successfully taken steps to improve their health prospects by either starting a healthy behavior or stopping an unhealthy one, and who have sustained the health-benefiting effort. Prochaska's research has also been used to create programs that support this action on a broader scale.

What have researchers learned? Their findings are summarized in Figure 7.2. The first finding is that

people often change themselves successfully, if inefficiently. They stop smoking, moderate their drinking, lose weight, become regular exercisers, and they do it on their own. And these changes can stick for long periods of time, if not for good. More importantly, the research revealed factors that consistently correspond to these successful examples of change. Researchers have learned there are stages people typically go through in the process of self-change. And they've learned there are techniques that are particularly appropriate for the stage(s) an individual is in, which can make the process of change more "efficient."

Finally, researchers note that successful techniques for change are "trans-theoretical" – they borrow from several theories of psychology and apply what works

Figure 7.2: What Behavioral Health Researchers Have Learned

- People often change themselves successfully, if inefficiently.
- There are factors that consistently correspond to these successful examples of change.
- There are stages people typically go through in the process of self-change.
- There are techniques that are particularly appropriate for the stage(s) an individual is in, and that can make the process more "efficient."
- These recommended techniques are integrated or "trans-theoretical" – they borrow from several theories of psychology and apply what works to the specific stage.

(Prochaska et. al, 2006)

to the specific stage. In other words, *an integrated approach is the most effective pathway to achieving a sustained improvement in behavior.*

In *The Power of Sustainable Thinking*, Bob Doppelt offers a five-stage approach to climate, environmental, and social welfare change efforts. His book, I believe, was the first direct and credible attempt to apply the findings of behavioral change research, which we are discussing here, to the world of sustainability and social change (Doppelt 2008, 72-76).

Doppelt and the scholastic predecessors he draws upon have identified three conditions (See Figure 7.3) that need to be in place for someone to change behavior in an enduring fashion. They have to do with discomfort or tension due to one's current state, a clear and significant benefit to taking a particular action that would relieve that discomfort, and confidence that the action (and relief) can be achieved.

Figure 7.3: Three Conditions for Lasting Behavioral Change

1. Sufficient tension between existing state and important unmet values and aspirations
2. Benefits of making the change must be seen to outweigh downsides
3. Adequate confidence in ability to close the gap and resolve the tension

(Doppelt 2008, 70-79)

In the green building movement, I think we've been better at creating or illuminating the first condition, not so great with the second, and pretty lacking regarding the third.

With the *first* condition, we've been good at describing the problem, but less adept at identifying unmet values and aspirations. In this case, I think we make assumptions about what people care about. In Chapter 6, I discussed *witnessing*, the method of non-partisan observing. That skill can come in handy in truly understanding what people actually care about. No judgment, no blaming, just discovery.

With the *second* condition, we in the green building movement have begun to understand that we need to make a case, i.e. that the benefits outweigh the costs – but if we don't understand what people care about, the case we make can be founded on false assumptions. For example, there's been an assumption that building/development is always about the money, and we've spent a lot of energy trying to make a case from this basis. In fact, our reliance on simplistic "payback" arguments has gotten us in trouble. There are people involved in any project who *only* want to know the bottom line, even if they will probably be better served with a true accounting that considers net present value and the like. I'm not a financial wizard, but my point is that for those who need this information, we should provide the data they care about, in language they understand. (See pioneer in the field of finance and sustainability Molly McCabe's contribution to this conversation in her essay: "Reframing the Real Estate Conversation So It Means Something," page 52.)

And not every decision is about the money. Have you heard anyone ask about the payback on their granite countertop? Often there are deeper motivations that you can *discover* by truly listening. Servant leader scholars refer to deep listening as "listening

Reframing the Real Estate Conversation So It Means Something

By Molly McCabe, MBA, Author, Management Consultant

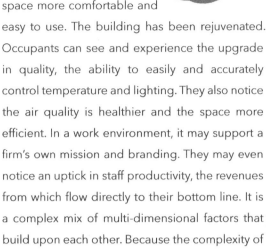

Real estate is an art, not a science. In any new venture (and this applies to renovation as well as new construction) the developer has a vision of what they want to create and must believe it will succeed. They are risking their own money and putting their reputation on the line, and in the process they are making calculated guesses on what will be most meaningful to the people who will use the space. The granite counter top has value because it implies something about the space and the builder. It sets the tone for the entire home. Marble in the lobby says something different than exposed brick. It sends a message of quality and sets the tone for the building. Similar things can be inferred from green components.

A true accounting of value incorporates these contributing factors in the analysis. They inform and speak to: the risk/return profile (e.g. capitalization and discount rates); the durability of the income stream (rent and expenses); the duration of occupancy (tenant attraction, retention and turnover costs); and the reputation and legacy (the quality of management, branding and commitment to craft).

Simple payback as the gatekeeper for investment is an inadequate measure of value. Take energy efficiency for example. Modernizing an existing building to optimize its efficiency generally means upgrading systems, better lighting, greater thermal comfort, and enhanced controls. These upgrades provide value to the occupant far above the expense savings derived from reduced energy use – i.e. they make the space more comfortable and easy to use. The building has been rejuvenated. Occupants can see and experience the upgrade in quality, the ability to easily and accurately control temperature and lighting. They also notice the air quality is healthier and the space more efficient. In a work environment, it may support a firm's own mission and branding. They may even notice an uptick in staff productivity, the revenues from which flow directly to their bottom line. It is a complex mix of multi-dimensional factors that build upon each other. Because the complexity of value is difficult to articulate without listening to stakeholders and learn what is important, simple payback becomes the default gatekeeper.

Reframe the conversation to incorporate language the people you are engaging understand. Listen for the words they use and probe for the underlying concepts. *Using Prochaska's terminology, this allows you to influence them to move from pre-contemplation to action.* For example, what drives the value of an asset? For an income producing property, value is generally centered in net operating income (e.g. rent and expenses) and asset appreciation. Income is generated when tenants occupy the space and pay their rent. What makes a tenant stay and what makes them pay a higher rent? It is qualitative – and rarely rests on one aspect. Incentives include total cost of occupancy – rental rate and operating expenses (e.g. utility costs, common area maintenance), the comfort and utility of space, amenities

Reframing the Real Estate Conversation So It Means Something *(Continued)*

(bike storage, health club, green space), location, management responsiveness and skill, transit options, and safety and security. And of course there is how it stacks up against the competition – hip and cool, or tired and worn down.

People are generally more willing to hear you out if you understand their situation and can reflect it back in their language. Being fluent in the concepts and the language around return on investment, net present value, asset repositioning, mitigation of risk, and enhancement of returns not only fleshes out your understanding of the issue, but also adds credibility when speaking with an investor or real estate owner. ✒

---

to the listening." We emergent leaders need to learn more about what a particular individual, client, or community group cares about, which requires we listen not just with our ears, but also with our eyes, minds, and hearts!

Finally, I think we've done a poor job of instilling confidence in the ability to make the change successfully, the *third* condition. It's not enough to enthuse about someone else's changing, or about the reason for someone to change – even if you are a respected, credible leader. The individual who is being invited to change needs to have a reasonable chance of succeeding at it in order to be willing to take a meaningful stab at it. Remember the last time you attended a keynote with an inspiring, knowledgeable speaker one day, and by the time you hit the office

the following Monday morning your willingness to apply the speaker's ideas had evaporated? *Inspiration without confidence is fantasy.*

The Change Continuum

As noted above, there are stages people typically go through in the process of self-change. I've listed these stages as presented by Prochaska in Figure 7.4.

Figure 7.4: Stages of Change

- Pre-contemplation
- Contemplation
- Preparation
- Action
- Maintenance
- Relapse

(Prochaska et. al, 2006)

Doppelt, as part of his interpretation of Prochaska's findings, created a variation on this list of attitudinal stages, a "5-D" continuum, that ranges from *disinterest to defending*, with "defending" identified as the stance taken when you have a change-plan in place and you are "defending" it against backsliding. (Figure 7.5) I've appreciated Doppelt's pioneering work importing behavioral science into the realm of sustainable social change. However, when I've described the change

Figure 7.5: Doppelt's 5-D Stages of Change

- Disinterest
- Deliberating
- Design
- Doing
- Defending

(Doppelt 2008, 77)

continuum/process in my workshops using Doppelt's terminology, I've received significant pushback, in particular with the use of the terms "disinterest" and "defending." The language Prochaska uses for these stages - "pre-contemplation" and "maintenance" - seems to resonate with some in a way that Doppelt's does not. I've resorted to providing both sets of terms, allowing my audience to use the one that works best for them.

Regardless of which term you use for the first stage (Doppelt's "disinterest" vs. Prochaska's "pre-contemplation") I believe this first stage is more nuanced than mere blissful ignorance, although I have seen it identified as such in derivative summaries of the concept. And, for my part, I believe the term "pre-contemplation" allows for more nuance than does "disinterest." I explain it this way: Have you ever felt like something was not quite right, but you didn't know what was wrong? So perhaps the "pre-contemplation" stage has two tiers - *tier 1*: blissful ignorance, and *tier 2*: annoyed but still ignorant!

Here's an example. Mary Jane has asthma, and she smokes. She hasn't even considered smoking as the source of her troubles because she's in denial - she doesn't smoke "*that* much." She might move to Arizona for better, drier weather, still smoking. She might take medication to control her asthma, still smoking. She's not disinterested in change. She's suffering and knows she's suffering, and is taking some action to cease the suffering. However, she hasn't yet determined (or admitted) that it's the smoking that's the problem. No, in her mind, the asthma is the problem. In my mind, she's pre-contemplating (or perhaps one might say she's processing the problem on an unconscious

level). This pre-contemplative state is very different from *knowing she has asthma and doing nothing about it* (which I would call disinterest). One day, she has a moment of clarity. It's the smoking! She begins to consciously contemplate how she might reduce or eliminate the problem, that is, how she can quit smoking.

Another example may be closer to home. John Mark's really annoyed at the fact that the local utility company is planning to build a new power plant near him, because it will spoil his view. He writes letters to the local newspaper and his legislators, and he attends a protest. For him, it's all about the view. He hasn't really identified the core issue: i.e. the new power plant is being built to satisfy energy needs he's a part of creating. Something's not right, but he doesn't know what's wrong (and that he is actually a part of the problem). If he's lucky, at one of the protests, there's a table with information on home energy efficiency and solar panels. He connects the dots and begins contemplating (or using Doppelt's terminology, deliberating) whether upgrading his home is worth it. If yes, he decides how he will accomplish this task, does it, and then defends it (that is, maintains the changes and operate his home in a way that's in keeping with his new energy efficient persona).

I would not waste my time with those who are disinterested, but might invest time in those who are pre-contemplating, so it's a nuance of language, and correlated behavior, worth considering.

Figure 7.6 illustrates the change process in a more visual format (adapted from Figure 1, Prochaska et.al. 2006, 49).

Six Stages of Change

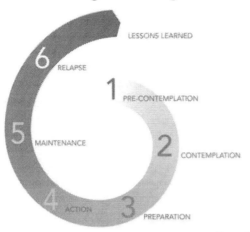

Figure 7.6

Once again, notice that relapse is part of the process. Although Doppelt recognizes it as part of the process (he calls it "backsliding"), he doesn't elevate it to an actual stage in the process (Doppelt 2008, 82). It *is* inconvenient, and can be extremely disappointing to someone trying to influence the change or be changed. "Setbacks may make you feel as though you are going around in circles rather than solving your problem. And, to some extent, that is the case, but the good news" says Prochaska, "is that the circles are spiraling upward." He adds: "Most successful self-changers go through the stages three or four times before they make it to the top and finally exit the cycle" (Prochaska et. al. 2006, 48).

In Chapter 2, I discussed my preference for using spiral imagery rather than linear imagery to describe progression towards our vision. The spiral evokes a multi-perspective and expansive learning process, which allows lessons to come through the open "empty" space of the spiral. That is, through the spiral information flows from above and below (or from imagination and experience). By including "relapse"

as a stage in the change process, Prochaska gives us permission to take risks, make mistakes, and know that we are still progressing towards our vision.

Techniques to Influence Behavioral Change

The attitudinal spectrum of change (whether you use Prochaska's terms or Doppelt's) is a helpful tool. As mentioned earlier, there are techniques that are more effective at some points along the spectrum and less effective elsewhere. (These are summarized in Figure 7.7.)

Knowing where someone (or a group of "someones") is on the attitudinal spectrum can help you outline a

Figure 7.7: Behavioral Mechanisms Related to Stages

- Early Stages (e.g. pre-contemplation): Emphasize cognitive reframing and experiential expansion
  - Consciousness-raising
  - Guided discussion
  - Emotional relief through role-playing
- Later Stages (e.g. planning or action): Emphasize behavioral mechanisms and skill building
  - Prompts for "good" behavior (Rewards, Penalties)
- Always: Emphasize supportive networks and relationships
  - Public pledges
  - Public affirmation of progress
  - Support groups
  - Buddy systems, Mentors

(Doppelt 2008, 87-125)

plan for change, which will include matching the most effective technique for a given situation.

Behavioral research has revealed that *cognitive reframing* is a good technique when addressing an individual in the early steps of a desired change. Cognitive reframing consists of identifying and then disputing "irrational" or "maladaptive thoughts." Reframing is a way of viewing and experiencing events, ideas, concepts and emotions to identify more positive alternatives ("Cognitive Reframing" June 30, 2015). In the case of our fictional John Mark, cognitive reframing could be accomplished through a form of inquiry such as: "Do you know how much energy you could save by doing 'x'? And do you know how much energy the community could save if everyone did 'x'? And do you know that if this were to happen the new power plant could be smaller or not 'have to be' built at all?"

According to Doppelt, "cognitive reframing constitutes the foundation of the entire process of altering personal, team and organizational thinking and behaviours regarding the climate, natural environment and social well-being. Cognitive reframing involves seeing our core belief, assumptions and automatic thoughts in a new light" (Doppelt 2008, 80).

Expanding someone's horizons through experience is also very helpful in the early stages. Tours of green projects (such as my own home) – where people could see, touch, and smell (or not smell, as in the case of non-toxic interior choices) the healthful options – have been a significant influence in getting to where we are today. Experience with on-the-ground green projects continues to be a major factor in helping people who

are open to green building move from contemplation to planning or even further along in the continuum.

Behavioral mechanisms such as prompts for good behavior are more helpful in the later stages of the change continuum. Rebates for desired behavior or contingency fees due for undesired behavior are examples of techniques that could act as such prompts. Offering a discount on that villa in Florida doesn't really move me much, unless I'm unhappy with where I am, I'm open to moving, *and* I think a warm climate might be something I want!

Providing supportive relationships is a critical behavioral mechanism appropriate throughout the change process, one of the reasons the EMERGE Leadership Model includes Community as one of its three key components.

Whatever techniques you are inspired to use, keep in mind that it is critical that the technique activate the behavioral mechanism appropriate for the stage, or it will essentially be a waste of time, energy (and probably money). In addition, nothing will happen if the conditions for change (discussed at the outset of this chapter) are not present.

Conscious Change For Leadership

The emergent leader is transparent about his or her intent to influence others to change. The best way to maintain transparency is to apply this process yourself and share both the process and the results. Can you create the conditions for change in some aspect of your own life? Can you consciously travel through the spiral? Do you have a relapse story? Your experience makes your desire to change the paths of organizations and communities authentic.

Think about a personal behavior you've changed (or would like to change). Why did/do you want to change? What generated that first inkling of considering change? Did you read a book, watch a documentary, have or adopt a child? What's the "wrong" feeling you wanted to "right?" How did you identify the problem? If you've made the change, what made the change seem worth it? Did someone you trust make a compelling case? What was compelling about it? How did they know it would be compelling for you? If you haven't made the change, what will your situation look like if you do change? It better look better, or you won't do it! What do you need to do in order to feel confident to do so? Find an ally? A mentor? Your experience of change, and in particular your understanding of what it takes to accomplish this change, is transferable data.

As important as it is to have a clear vision for social change, your own willingness to grow and experience change is perhaps even more critical. It gives you credibility. You can tell your own stories of change. More than that, it gives you a much better understanding of the change process than any book! The point I want to make is that if you can be mindful while making personal change, you will be equipped with important and valuable information when working with others. And happily this awareness can provide you with the confidence to be the leader you want to be (the third condition)!

Bill O'Brien, CEO of Hanover Insurance (and no relation), has been quoted saying, "The success of an intervention depends on the interior condition of the intervener" (Scharmer and Kaufer 2013, 18). Have no doubt, as an agent of social change we are intervening! (I'll discuss more about intervention in Chapter 8.)

I encourage anyone desiring to be an emergent leader to start and sustain a daily awareness practice that taps into something greater than yourself, whatever form that practice might take. It can be as simple as asking the question, "How can I be of service today?" and pausing to hear the answer. Whatever the practice, be it physical (walking or running) or a more contemplative practice (sitting in formal meditation, reading inspiring literature, journaling), a regular opportunity to quiet the mind can reduce anxiety, increase your ability to hear what your intuition has to say, and help you be more productive.

Combining physical and contemplative methods works well for me. I get cardio, core, and flextime through yoga, lap swimming (or walking), and weight training, with an average of one hour of physical exercise a day. My day begins with a 20-minute session that includes reading spiritual works, writing, and quiet. I use my smart phone's timer to help me stay put! Then I like to end the day with a brief mental review, identifying things I might have done better, things that went well, and closing with a grateful review of the gifts I've received throughout the day, whether they are opportunities to act or simply an experience of a feeling. (Friends I know make a "gratitude list" each night.)

I don't expect you to start project meetings by leading the team in meditative chants; however, if you maintain a regular awareness practice, I guarantee it will transform the way you act and the way you approach decisions. This will intrigue your peers, employees, or clients, especially those who are interested in growing themselves. Sharing what you are doing, when asked, or in formal mentoring relationships, can be incredibly satisfying.

Three Keys to Change

We will continue to look at the Change component of the EMERGE Leadership Model in the next few chapters, with more discussion about what it takes to create the systemic change we are hoping for, as well as the issue of creating the "will" to change. We'll also look at the process of *integrative design* as a change management process. It's useful to conclude this chapter, however, with what Doppelt considers the three keys to successful change: know the stage of change and use appropriate change mechanisms; (consciously) build tension for change and enhance the belief in the prospective changer their ability to achieve the change; and emphasize benefits early on and deal with downsides in the later stages of change (Doppelt 2008, 77-80).

How to Intervene in Systems

Systems theory is the centerpiece of the Change component of the EMERGE Leadership Model (Figure 8.1).

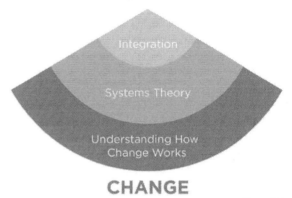

Figure 8.1

Now that we know there are certain conditions necessary for change and certain techniques to both create those conditions and foster the desired change, it would be tempting to think formulaically about leading a change process. Such thinking would ignore, at least, a couple of things. As I have stressed earlier, you are not actually in control of the outcome! An emergent leader works to foster conditions for a positive outcome, but can't dictate the results. In my experience, taking a "controlling" posture may actually *reduce* the likelihood of arriving at the best outcomes and *increase* the likelihood of undesirable unintended consequences.

The other downside of a less-than-mindful, lock-step approach to leading change is the potential to miss the opportunity to grow leaders who themselves desire to serve (that is, to practice servant leadership). And, consequently, one may miss out on the opportunity to create a leadership dynamic that would better ensure positive momentum towards the larger vision.

Approaching *change work* like you would a cake recipe ignores the fact that we are working within and upon systems. In *Thinking in Systems*, Meadows wrote, "We can't impose our will on a system. We can listen to what the system tells us, and discover how its properties and our values can work together to bring forth something much better than could ever be produced by our will alone" (Meadows 2006, 169-170).

With that caveat in mind, it has been useful in working with clients on change projects to consider the following means of intervention: education, rewarding policy, penalizing policy, and mandates. (Figure 8.2)

Figure 8.2: Strategic Means of Intervention

- Educate: Raise Awareness/Advocate.
- Rewarding Policy: Make it convenient to do the right thing.
- Penalizing Policy: Make it inconvenient to do the wrong thing.
- Mandate: Make it illegal to do the wrong thing.

In the U.S. we rely heavily on education and mandates. (Depending on the politics of a community, we might lean more on education, or more on mandates.) Convenient/inconvenient policy levers are used much less frequently and for shorter durations. In a capitalist society these policies are politicized as undeserved "gifts" or punishments. And of course, as I discussed earlier, there are policies that are ostensibly protecting the public that actually make it inconvenient or even illegal to do the *right* thing! (A significant portion of the Bullitt Center project's transformative power has been in highlighting this reality by pushing against policies regarding waste water treatment and potable water supply. See the Bullitt Center "Transformation in Practice," earlier.)

Regardless of the method used, it is extremely important to be leveraging the outcome you actually desire. Prescriptive energy codes are a great example of the danger of unwittingly causing unintended consequences. While the writers of these codes hope to raise the bar, in practice they set the ceiling. I have witnessed appalling discussions where project teams hoped to "game" the system in order to get the maximum amount of glazing in a building (which translates into the maximum allowable heat or cool loss)! Prescriptive codes – which tend to be the default pathway, even when a systems path is available – generally do not stimulate innovation, at least not in a positive direction.

I've seen similar tactics in LEED workshops, especially when LEED was a requirement and the conditions for change discussed in Chapter 6 were lacking. How many of you have been witness to a discussion of a particular LEED point, when the action that would earn the credit is meaningless in the context of a particular project? For example, installing a bike rack on an industrial project which -- for good reason -- is located out in the middle of nowhere? In the vernacular of LEED teams, this is "buying a point." It's heartening to see interest in and movement toward performance language in LEED and other green building standards and codes, but as emergent leaders we need something more.

That something more is a *strategic framework* applied to our leadership. Rather than trying to change everything at once, e.g. with a one-size-fits-all mandate, Wheatley encourages us to "generate energy in one area, then watch what the networks do with our work" (Wheatley 2006, 153). We apply this advice when we stimulate activity by providing early adopters with what they need to succeed with a particular approach (preferably performance-based, but not always), with the goal of inspiring the early majority (and perhaps even the late majority!) to follow suit, and thus moving the mainstream toward a tipping point. This process is systemic change at its most effective.

The point is that we need to be strategic about how we work, looking for the just the right place(s) – the "hot" spots, so to speak – to do our work. And we also need to be strategic *with* whom we work. (Note Sidebar asking the question: "Should We Preach to the Choir?" page 62.)

In her discussion of "systems wisdom" (see Figure 8.3) Donella Meadows advises us to "study the beat" of systems before we "disturb the system in any way" (Meadows 2006, 170), so we can better leverage the right outcomes. We want to avoid rewarding undesired actions, and punishing desired actions.

When hoping to intervene in a system, we need to apply the resources we have in a way that has meaning to the system. In their book, *Switch: How To Change*

Figure 8.3: Wisdom Advice for Systems Thinkers

- Get the beat of the system
- Expose your mental models to the light of day
- Honor, respect, and distribute information
- Use language with care and enrich it with systems concepts
- Pay attention to what is important not just what is quantifiable
- Make feedback policies for feedback systems
- Go for the good of the whole
- Listen to the wisdom of the system
- Locate responsibility in the system
- Stay humble – stay a learner
- Celebrate complexity
- Expand time horizons
- Defy the disciplines
- Expand the boundary of caring
- Don't erode the goal of goodness

(Drawn from Meadows 2006, Chapter 7)

Things When Change Is Hard, in which Chip and Dan Heath discuss how we can "switch" the thinking and therefore the behavior of others', they emphasize this point: *"Any change effort that violates someone's identity is likely doomed to failure"* (Heath 2010, 154).

Listening for Meaning

How do we know what is meaningful to a particular person, organization, or system? We must listen, listen, listen, as Scharmer, Meadows, Wheatley, and Greenleaf have been telling us in any number of ways! If we don't listen, we won't know what actions have meaning to a given system (and to the players

Should We Preach to the Choir?

I think a word about "preaching to the choir" is in order. Often this phrase is used disparagingly or dismissively, with the implication that we should be focusing our change work on people who need to be convinced. In a workshop I attended in February 2014 on writing with a social purpose in mind, Kathleen Dean Moore, author (and former Distinguished Professor of Philosophy at the University of Oregon) made an excellent observation regarding this point. When someone raised the chronic complaint "Aren't we just preaching to the choir with our socially motivated writing?" Dean noted that most choirs (and having sung in a church choir for ten years I can vouch for this) represent a mix of motivations and abilities. At times some choir members are confused, maybe they don't know how to read music and have lost their place. Some members may be hypocrites – singing in the choir makes them look good. Some folks have great singing voices, but they like to "show off" and don't behave well when blending is required for harmony's sake. You get the picture. Dean Moore also observed that although data indicates that a majority of Americans believe in climate change, a majority of Americans don't believe we should prioritize the issue. Like the choir, they are confused, or they may be hypocrites. And I would add that those with special knowledge and talent in regard to climate change may have difficulty "blending with others."

On this subject, Wheatley believes that "'preaching to the choir' is exactly the right thing to do" because of the way networks work with energy (Wheatley 2006, 151).

This is not to say we should ignore those who don't seem to be in the choir - just that we should be cautious. At our EMERGE Leadership workshops, EMERGE Faculty and DCAT Executive Director David Eisenberg often talks about spending some time with individuals who need to be convinced (understanding that we may be only one in a line of influencers that might impact this person's ideas and actions) - but not too much. He warns against spending your personal leadership currency on what he terms "black holes." It can wear you out with very little result.

within the system). As emergent leaders practicing servant leadership competencies, we offer receptive, non-judgmental listening, i.e. hearing the content of a communication – nothing more, nothing less – and responding to what is actually said. We let go of ignoring, pretending, controlling (through gestures or sounds for example), and projecting (through completing someone else's sentences), and begin respecting, empathizing. Our listening becomes more sophisticated. We practice active listening with the goal of evoking the best qualities in others.

Earlier, I referred to a practice encouraged by servant-leader scholars – "listening to the listening" – where you practice listening to how others are listening to you. What questions are your "listeners" asking you when you are communicating your ideas, your vision? What non-verbal communication signals are *they* sending as they listen? As an emergent leader we become aware of how our words and other communications are received. Without this level of sophistication, we are merely making assumptions about what our audience actually cares about.

Reframing the Issue

In Chapter 7 we discussed *cognitive reframing* as a type of behavioral mechanism to consider right from the first stages of a change project. Doppelt provides some examples of cognitive reframing including disturbances, emotional inspiration, awareness-building, and self-appraisal (Doppelt 2008, 81). All of these methods (at times arrived at intuitively, at times arrived at logically) are exemplified in the development of Built Green Santa Barbara. (The program's logo is shown in Figure 8.4.)

Figure 8.4

Al Gore's disturbing documentary "An Inconvenient Truth" on climate change and Ed Mazria's inspiring and riveting talk on the same subject, as well as Mazria's Architecture 2030 Challenge to solve the problem – were part of a long process of cognitive reframing that influenced the Santa Barbara Contractor Association's leadership to conceive of itself as a leader in green building, rather than as "cogs" in a wheel.

Well before the showing of "*An Inconvenient Truth*" and Mazria's keynote, the green building movement had quietly begun in the area with a series of questions that invited self-appraisal. Joe Campanelli, one of the early adopters of green building in the region, (and later one of the founders of Built Green Santa Barbara) shared recently in a phone conversation: "I was invited in 1999 to present on a green commercial office building I was planning. I hadn't even started construction, so I didn't really have much to report, but I did hope to raise awareness, and I had a lot of questions. I remember asking: 'What would it take to move from concept to reality? With regard to green building, do we want to be at the table influencing policy, creating this reality? Because it's not a matter of if, but when'" (Campanelli, July 6, 2015). Joe's questions – and later his video of the project, "Diary of a Green Building" – helped stimulate self-examination on the part of those attending and a conversation that eventually led the Santa Barbara Contractors Association to investigate the Built Green program model. Climate change, energy efficiency, water conservation all became relevant to the industry member. It had entered their frame of reference. I had the privilege of working with the group to develop their version of Built Green, which continues to this day, offering contractor accountability tools and training, as well as public education. Thanks to Joe and his colleagues at the SBCA, the industry has been part of the solution, knowledgeably and substantively influencing local policy and environmental activism.

Whether a book, film, keynote, or conversation is depressing or inspiring, the resulting disturbance is the sense of an awareness that things, as they are, are not in alignment with things as they should be. The disturbance helps illuminate the tension between existing conditions and values – it helps create the first condition for change.

As emergent leaders we need to maintain awareness of the "wholeness" of a system, while we are focusing on specific aspects of the system. Like Meadows, who exhorts us to "listen to the beat," Wheatley urges us to avoid being overly analytical, especially since, as quantum mechanics tells us, every time we "measure" something, we actually interfere. This is not to say that measurement is wrong, we just need to be aware of this interference phenomenon, and we must balance measurement with intuitive perception. "Instead of the ability to analyze and predict, we need to know how to stay acutely aware of what's happening now, and we need to be better...learners from what just happened" (Wheatley 2006, 38). This acute awareness brings to mind our earlier discussion of foresight in Chapter 5. Once again we find this characteristic of a servant leader – and emergent leader by extension - quite

pertinent. Systems theory tells us that logic alone will not be enough. Logic and analytic thinking is of course useful, but particularly in a systemic environment, we need to be able to access our intuition to identify where in the system we should intervene, and how.

Focusing the energy for intervention

Since we *don't* have unlimited time and resources, and we *do* want to be strategic, we should be looking at the most effective leverage points in the systems we are hoping to transform. Meadows gave us a dozen of such leverage points in her famous essay "Places to Intervene in a System." As Figure 8.5 illustrates, she ranked as extremely poor in terms of effectiveness the kinds of interventions that employ technologies and tools, for example, taxes, subsidies, and feedback regulators (positive and negative). From her commentary one can infer that even the "best" technologies and tools are worthless (or even harmful) if they successfully drive change in the wrong direction. As Lance Hosey (Chief Sustainability Officer and Principal at Perkins Eastman) has pointedly complained, "Technology has hijacked sustainability... believing new tools will solve the problem is like

Figure 8.5: Places to Intervene in a System *(In increasing order of effectiveness)*

12. Constants, parameters, numbers (such as subsidies, taxes, standards)
11. The sizes of buffers and other stabilizing stocks, relative to their flows
10. The structure of material stocks and flows (such as transport networks, population age structures)

continued on next page

Figure 8.5 (continued)

9. The lengths of delays, relative to the rate of system change

8. The strength of negative feedback loops, relative to the impacts they are trying to correct against

7. The gain around driving positive feedback loops

6. The structure of information flows (who does and does not have access to information)

5. The rules of the system (such as incentives, punishments, constraints)

4. The power to add, change, evolve, or self-organize system structure

3. The goals of the system

2. The mindset or paradigm out of which the system – its goals, structure, rules, delays, parameters – arises

1. The power to transcend paradigms

(Meadows 1999)

Figure 8.6: Places to Intervene in a System *(In increasing order of effectiveness)*

4. Technologies
3. Tools
2. Process
1. Mindset

(Reed and Batshalom 2005)

thinking better needles will help someone kick a heroin habit" (Hosey 2013).

For those of us who find it hard to juggle a dozen concepts in our head at the same time, Barbara Batshalom and Bill Reed of Regenesis Group and the Integrative Design Collaborative offered a simplification of Meadows' theory in an article for the Environmental Building News (Malin 2005, 128). One of the neat things about this simplification is that it makes it easier to apply, regardless of the size of the system you are hoping to affect, whether you are thinking about a two-person design firm, or a community with a population in the thousands.

In Figure 8.6, I've used the magic of font sizes to emphasize the order of effectiveness with mindset and process as the top choices followed by tools then technologies. The fact that mindset rates top billing makes understanding the psychology of change even more important. The fact that process is right behind it makes understanding how to better align our vision and process through integrative design just as important. Before we go on however, I'd like to note that systems theory and thinking is an incredibly complex topic of which we have just skimmed the surface (both in our discussion of the Leadership component of the EMERGE Leadership Model, and now the Change component). I will not pretend nor try to cover the subject in depth. (My sources are listed in References if you wish to read more on the subject.) For the purposes of this book, however, I'm providing a quick glossary of some key systems terms. (Figure 8.7, page 66.)

Figure 8.7: Quick Glossary of Systems Terms

- System: Something that requires all of itself to do its thing. It has multiple elements, they are connected, and it has a purpose or function.
- Feedback: The dynamic that makes a system run "by itself."
  - Positive feedback: Self-reinforcing (vicious/virtuous)
  - Negative feedback: Self-correcting (balancing)
- Model: Everything we know about a (the) world.
  - Mental Model: How I picture that world in my head
  - It may have a strong congruence with the world but falls short of representing the world fully
- Lever Point: Where a participant in a system can change the behavior of the system.
- Intervention: When a participant (or outsider) in a system tries to change the behavior of the system.

(Meadows 2008 and others)

Developing the Will to Do the Right Thing

As we've discussed, behavioral research has illuminated the conditions required for change. It can also tell us how we can best foster these conditions. To review those conditions, they include: tension between the way things are and the way you think or feel they should be given your values; the benefits of the change outweigh the downsides; and sufficient confidence exists that the change can be successfully accomplished.

In *Flourish*, Seligman presents the finding that performance increases with morale, and that one aspect of a healthy morale (or "fitness") is optimism. Because of this relationship between morale and performance, "the cultivation of happiness," which he says is badly neglected, is "important, perhaps crucial" (Seligman 2011, 146). Not in the Pollyanna sense that defeat is denied or ignored! Rather, defeat should be seen as temporary and an opportunity to learn and build resilience. So it is extremely important when highlighting or stimulating the tension between what is and what could be, that it be done in tandem with building confidence that that gap *can* be closed.

One of the reasons the EMERGE Leadership Model includes a Community Component is that social science research tells us we are much more likely to succeed using a *we can* approach, not a *you must –* or worse, *you are wrong and must atone –* approach. To borrow from U.S. Army Strong training literature, a program Seligman was instrumental in designing, "Human survival depends on our collective abilities, our ability to join together with others in pursuing a goal, not on our individual might. The cohesiveness and social resilience of the group...matters" (Seligman, 2011, 145). The lack of sustainability in our built environment and in our society in general is a "we" problem, and we must (and really can only) solve it, in community.

Shrinking the Gap

In *Switch*, brothers Chip and Dan Heath reveal some surprising facts about change identified in recent social research. By understanding this information, they believe we can more easily influence others to change. Most pertinent to this discussion is their report of the finding that what looks like laziness is often exhaustion! (Heath 2010, 12). I have definitely seen designers, builders, project managers, and building officials struggling with *overwhelm*. Perhaps their resistance to changing the way they might approach a project (for example, add an investigation of Living Building certification to the work-plan) may look to some, such as their supervisor, colleague or client, as disinterest or laziness. If we can't add more hours to the day, more dollars to the budget, to address this feeling, what can be done? Among other remedies, the Heaths suggest "shrinking" the gap between current conditions and desired conditions (Heath 2012, 124). Perhaps prioritizing one petal in the Living Building Standard for this project is in order, or offering some free professional education on the topic of Living Building – a work/stress reducer only if the individual has a professional CEU deadline coming up!

Doing the right thing can be difficult when for one reason or another one's willpower is depleted.

Yes. It may surprise you, but willpower is a finite resource. Stress and over-relying on self-control, for example, can tax this personal resource (McGonigal 2012, 56-57). Kelly McGonigal references this and other behavioral research to help individuals use their willpower to change themselves for the better. In *The Willpower Instinct*, McGonigal discusses how one can use the willpower instinct to meet willpower challenges. When fatigue or other factors deplete one's willpower and desire to "do the right thing," she advises using "choice architecture" that will make it easier for you to choose the "better" thing. An example she gives is automatic scheduling of checkups (McGonigal 2011, 78). Think about how this might apply to our Living Building project example above. Including a regular item on the weekly project meeting agenda, and not relegating it to the end of the agenda, might be a way to keep this aspiration front and center. (True confession: I bring chocolate to afternoon meetings where we're asking the participants to go the extra mile.)

As the emergent leader, shrinking the gap would also include looking more critically at how you are describing the scope of the problem and the actions you are hoping for. Are you trying to address the lack of affordable housing built with sustainable features? That may be the vision that is driving you or your organization, but it's a big bite to digest as a practical matter. With your team, break the vision down into attainable goals and objectives that are relevant to the particular situation. For example, "In this project, all of our units will be built with sustainable features, and we want to make sure x percentage of units are available at prices that are affordable as defined by x." Later, you can celebrate how solving this particular problem is contributing to the larger vision.

Go Slow to Go Fast

The EMERGE Leadership Project hopes to accelerate progress toward the vision of a thriving planet. However, consider the phrase "go slow to go fast." Providing steps that are reasonable or gradual reduces exhaustion, and offers opportunities to review, regroup, and move on. For some reason, *incrementalism* has become a naughty word of late, with disparagers asserting that it means the lack of a great vision, just a creeping forward without a larger view to guide progress. But I'm a firm believer in incremental gains, outlining what they can be, and celebrating them when they occur.

In working with trade associations around the country to develop Built Green® and similar industry-based programs, there were contentious discussions about whether the rating systems should be pass-fail or tiered (i.e. have multiple rating levels). The latter won out, I'm glad to say, because it helped more conservative builders "try green building on for size." Often they were doing better than they thought, which made them open to try even more. Over and over, Built Green® program managers would tell me stories of contractors who thought a particular tier was as far as they could reasonably go. Yet when they found they were close to achieving the next tier, they would stretch themselves and advance. If these programs had been set up as pass-fail, there would have been no incentive to do better. And if the bar was set too low for pass-fail, the program would be little more than a public relations campaign.

Not all Built Green® programs have enjoyed the same level of success. I find it extremely interesting that the most vibrant have continued to raise the bar, both by increasing an emphasis on performance and by increasing the breadth of the programs. For example, the Built Green® Program of King and Snohomish County (Puget Sound Region/Washington), which has certified more than 20,000 projects in its territory, has over time removed the original bottom tier (the 1- star rating) and added two tiers (the 4 and 5-star ratings). These higher tiers require levels of performance and accountability that would have been completely unacceptable by industry members when we first created the program in the late 1990s. (I am certain that if we'd insisted on these requirements at that time, the program would have been dead on arrival.) This particular Built Green® program, which grew out of a desire to protect the industry from the "shock" of regulations pertaining to the 1999 EPA listing of Chinook salmon as endangered, very quickly, and to this day, continues to widen its lens to address other environmental and related social issues through its program. I believe that the simpler, easier versions of this and other programs have led the way to the more rigorous programs we are now seeing. The gap is shrinking – *incrementally!*

Providing Sufficient Meaning to the Change

We can reduce the feeling of "exhaustion" the Heaths point to by focusing on positive emotions, such as joy, curiosity, and pride. Recall Seligman's advice to foster optimism. Although pessimism can be used to infuse some reality into your thought process, too much can have a debilitating effect. The Heaths believe that to "create and sustain change, [a leader has] got to act more like a coach, and less like a scorekeeper.... [Understanding effort as a learning opportunity] reframes failure as a natural part of the change process. And [this reframing] is critical, because people will persevere only if they perceive falling down as learning rather than as failing" (Heath 2010, 168- 169).

Earlier, in Chapter 8, I shared the Heaths' admonition to honor the identity of anyone we are hoping to influence. In our work developing green building programs, it was important that the process and the product of our work recognize and encourage pride of craft, and draw on the fact that tradespeople simply enjoy being proud of their work. In addition, successful builders are savvy business owners. They'll want to know how participating in such a program makes good business sense. And many builders can be family-focused, with multi-generations participating in the business. They will enjoy knowing that their participation benefits their families, their neighbors' families, and future generations. How do we know what is meaningful to those we are hoping to influence? As mentioned previously, this has a lot to do with discovering what is meaningful through deep listening. (Surveys are a good start, but discovery in face-to-face conversations was how I learned any of the above about the contractors I was working with.)

The second condition for change requires us as influencers to make the case that the benefits of the desired change outweigh the downsides. This makes a lot of sense, of course, but there's an interesting tidbit from behavioral change research that Doppelt includes in *The Power of Sustainable Thinking*, and which really caught my attention. The research includes the finding that "to advance from the initial stage of disinterest to doing, an individual's perception of the benefits of new thinking and behaviour must increase by an average of one standard deviation.... In other words," Doppelt adds, "for every downside of change, people need to see at least two benefits" (Doppelt 2008, 79). It's quirkily quantitative. Benefits can be avoidance of harms, as well as positive gains. Doppelt argues that although some researchers feel the former carries a stronger clout, he has not seen this in practice. I would agree. What's more important is that the pros and cons must actually mean something to those you hope to influence (even if they might be of various weights "objectively"). Listening for the listening, discussed earlier in the book, will again be an important competency for the emergent leader who wishes to make a case that is compelling.

From reading the literature, it also becomes clear that making the case for change is not a one-time thing. Hence the Heaths' use of the term "coach" seems quite appropriate. As long as someone is willing to play, the coach has a role to play. Doppelt notes that as the person changing gets further into the process, there's more of a need to help that person overcome the downsides of the change, "because of the need people have to deal with resistance and surmount obstacles" (Doppelt 2008, 79).

It seems appropriate here to revisit the third condition for change to occur: *adequate confidence in the ability to succeed.* Earlier we discussed the Heaths' suggestion to shrink the gap between the current state and the desired state as one way to build confidence. Based on research that indicates that behind resistance is often a lack of clarity, the Heaths suggest we make the solutions we are suggesting understandable. "If you seek out a solution that's as complex as the problem... nothing will change" (Heath 2010, 15). The keep it simple rule applies.

As a systems thinker it will be your job to identify the points in a system where change is possible and illuminate them. There's a great story in *Switch* about Jerry Sternin, who in 1990 was working for Save the Children, and charged with finding a solution to childhood malnutrition in rural Vietnam. Thick reports written by NGOs on the complicated origins of child malnutrition had not made a dent in the problem. What did make a dent (and a huge one) was learning from mothers of children who were healthier (taller, heavier) what they were doing, and inviting those mothers, and providing them resources, to teach this information to their peers in that village, and eventually to mothers from other villages. The Heaths report that the overall improvement in height and weight indicators for children living in the original location was 65%. Mothers from more than 200 villages traveled to the first village for cooking lessons, expanding the benefit of this very simple solution exponentially. This story points out the benefit of *working with what's working* – that is, a lever point in the system – *making the change a matter of identity* (as in, being a good mom), *breaking the big change down into comprehensible steps*, and *rallying peer perception* (people care what other people do). The program was very effective and less expensive than the large scale solutions contained in those thick reports (Heath 2010, 27-31).

Tactics for Persuasion

As noted above, building someone's confidence to make a change is generally an incremental process. In *Influence: The Psychology of Persuasion*, Robert Cialdini cites six "tactics" that savvy marketers use to influence their audiences: reciprocation, commitment/consistency, social proof, liking, authority, and scarcity. Each tactic is based on a psychological principle that has evolved to preserve human society (Cialdini 2007). Of course, these tactics can be used for good or bad.

If you intend to create public relations or advocacy programs, you should definitely read Cialdini's book, but for now I'll briefly discuss just three of the psychological principles he covers to show how tactics based on these principles might be or have been used in situations that would be familiar to you.

Reciprocation: By virtue of the reciprocity principle, we are obligated to the future repayment of, for example, favors, gifts, or invitations. This is the principle at work in the now rare direct-mail campaigns in which you received a dollar bill along with a paper survey. If you accepted the dollar, you were more likely to complete and submit the survey. Community energy efficiency programs depend on this principle when they offer free energy audits, with the hope that this will lead to a more comprehensive energy performance test, and then to an energy-efficiency upgrade (Cialdini 2007, 17-18).

Liking: As a rule, we most prefer to say "yes" to requests from someone we know and like. That's how we end up at Tupperware® parties or purchasing a service from someone a friend has referred us to. Cialdini warns us that just throwing people together is not enough to create real liking. It can backfire, and create competitive and conflictive interactions, leading to "dislike." Better results have come about, says Cialdini, when a "jigsaw" approach is taken. The various players are pieces in an interactive "puzzle" that when they work together – and Cialdini discusses creating cooperative situations where they *have* to work together to solve a problem – the participants get to know and like each other (Cialdini 2007, 179-180). Sometimes this cooperation can be as simple as asking a project team to work together to create a better room layout for a planning meeting! Yes, I mean physically re- arranging tables and chairs.

An exercise I've led included providing a site questionnaire to participants in an eco-charette for a school construction project who were meeting for the first time. In addition to the design team, the group included educators, parents, and administrators. (Students were not invited for this meeting, but that would have been a good idea!) We had participants pair up with a clipboard, and they walked the site working to complete the questionnaire. In addition to bonding, this exercise had the benefit of providing important information to them as they were about to spend several hours prioritizing sustainability goals for the project. We also learned important information about what the participants themselves valued.

Commitment & Consistency: Underlying this tactic is the principle that once we have made a choice or taken a stand we will encounter personal and interpersonal pressures to behave consistently with that commitment. Those pressures will cause us to respond in ways that justify our earlier decision. Cialdini reports on a research project conducted in 1980 in Iowa that used what he termed a "lowball" procedure to influence homeowners to conserve energy. A control sample of homeowners who agreed to try to conserve were given energy conservation tips,

and nothing else. No real savings occurred. Another group of homeowners who agreed to save energy, by employing energy conservation tips, were promised their names would be printed in the newspaper, where they would be recognized as public-spirited, fuel-conserving citizens. After a month, and an average savings of more than 400 cubic feet of natural gas apiece, the promise to publicize their names was retracted with a letter of apology. At the end of the winter, utility records showed they'd conserved *more* fuel than they had during the time they thought they'd get public recognition. Their savings increased from 12.2% to 15%. The same experiment was conducted with summer air conditioning with even better results. These people had been convinced to make a conservation commitment through a promise of newspaper publicity. Once made, that commitment started generating its own support. Cialdini theorizes that these positive results were due to several reasons: the homeowners began acquiring new energy habits; they felt good about their public-spirited efforts; they became convinced themselves of the vital need to reduce American dependence on foreign fuel; they appreciated the monetary savings in their utility bills; they felt proud of their capacity for self-denial; and *most important*, they began viewing themselves as "conservation minded." The experiment built on their identity as "good citizens" to include being environmental stewards. One might wonder why they actually saved more once the promise for publicity was rescinded. Cialdini concludes that the promise for publicity didn't allow the homeowners to fully own the commitment, and once this outside incentive was removed, it "removed the only impediment to these residents' images of themselves as fully concerned, energy- conscious citizens" (Cialdini 2007, 100-102).

I'm not suggesting that you manipulate those you seek to lead, by promising, for example, something you know you won't provide. But it is helpful to understand the importance – and the potential – of providing opportunities to "try something on" that will lead to a lasting activity.

More recently I have benefited personally from Cialdini's expertise. He's a consultant to OPower, the software platform that utilities are using to help their residential customers compare themselves to neighbors in similar housing. My utility and the local energy efficiency program, Repower, cooperated to send me information about where I stood energy consumption-wise vis-à-vis my neighbors who live in similar-sized homes. My understanding from the local Repower Program Manager is that just by sending this information to homeowners in our community, there was a 2% drop in energy use. Given what Cialdini is telling us, once these customers find themselves on the "good" side of conservation, they will continue to behave in keeping with this new persona. They will be more likely, for example, to sign up for an energy audit, and thus be subject to the principle of reciprocation!

TRANSFORMATION IN PRACTICE:
The Seattle 2030 District

The Seattle 2030 District is another example of emergent leadership, in that it both catalyzes change while allowing itself to evolve in how it seeks to accomplish that goal. It is responsive to the stakeholders it serves, while being constructively proactive in its leadership. In addition, it has been instrumental in modeling and replicating the initiative elsewhere, acting as a mentor to other communities, sharing its lessons learned, while learning from those communities as well.

The District is a groundbreaking high performance area in downtown Seattle and the surrounding neighborhoods. It aims to help the City of Seattle meet its Climate Action Plan carbon reduction goals by improving energy performance and reducing carbon emissions through facility construction and operations. The 2030 District's territory overlaps to some extent with the South Lake Union District discussed elsewhere (see "Transformation in Practice: South Lake Union District"). (The illustration shows the area in white; participating buildings are shaded.)

The Seattle 2030 District is private-sector led with City cooperation. Members of the District are property owners of any-sized buildings within a designated area, in other words, businesses that directly compete with each other for tenants! The District members have committed to work together by sharing information about what they're doing to improve their buildings' energy performance and reduce water consumption. They also commit to sharing actual energy and water consumption data with 2030 District staff, who aggregate it and provide members with a report showing how they compare to similar buildings in the District (in size and use).

Not surprisingly, neighboring buildings in this area differ wildly in terms of energy and water consumption due to age, design, use, and other factors. As such, opportunities for conservation and carbon emissions reduction will also vary. By collaborating, members leverage resources and influence, which individually they could not do.

The District's founding members' intent was to showcase the City, increase the entire District's economic and environmental appeal, and obviate the need for regulation by achieving the City's carbon reduction goals voluntarily. They recognized that for some buildings stricter energy performance requirements could be quite onerous, while for others, not so much. By aggregating energy savings data, the group could achieve the desired results without "shaming" buildings (and their owners) that could not meet these regulations but nonetheless contributed to the downtown "green" scene.

The City of Seattle was one of the first of a nearly dozen cities that have enacted an energy benchmarking requirement. This action might have been challenging; however local utilities have helped by offering automated benchmarking services linking consumption data to the EPA's Energy Star Portfolio Manager® - a free on-line tool. So it's not too surprising that Seattle for the last two years has boasted 99% compliance with the City's benchmarking program requirements (City of Seattle, April 1, 2013, April 1, 2014).

This accomplishment is actually a big deal, because this kind of information is considered confidential and rarely shared. Currently, the City's ordinance does not ask that property owners share information with the world, just to make it available to tenants, lenders, and buyers et al., in confidential disclosures.

All involved with the District understand the adage that you successfully "manage what you measure," so this compliance *is* something to brag about. District staff recognize, however, that busy owners and property managers need help prioritizing and interpreting the data. "We try to make sure they are looking at the data, and reading it for 'red flags' like spikes in consumption," says Matthew Combe, the District's Program and Operations Director (Combe August 17. 2015).

Combe reports that 165 buildings, representing over 45% of the City's downtown square footage have joined the challenge since it began only four years ago. Combe points to success stories among District participants,

such as that of JSH Properties. According to the District's 2013 Annual Report, the firm manages six buildings in the District, built between 1929 and 1999 and comprising over 800K square feet (Seattle 2030 District 2014, 9).

"To kickstart their sustainability program, JSH chose to be a part the District's Strategic Energy Management (SEM) pilot. Their newly hired sustainability coordinator worked with the District to set a short-term energy savings target, develop an action plan to achieve those savings, and implement it. They ended up realizing significant savings across their portfolio in just one year" Combe August 17, 2015). Their First and Stewart Building (see photo), for example, experienced a nearly 16% reduction in energy use

(Seattle 2030 District 2014, 9).

The initiative must continue to evolve, however, to achieve its goals. "While the District's average energy consumption reduction for building operation and transport (including both District members and non-members) seems to be on track to meet its 2030 goals, water conservation numbers are low," says Combe. "This is primarily because we don't have the benefit of automated benchmarking (and, thus ease of data gathering) like we do with energy, so not as many owners and managers have integrated water reporting into their systems. The member buildings that *are* sharing their data are achieving 15% improvement in water efficiency. We think once we start capturing more of the data, we will see a 10% reduction over the average of all buildings in the District." The District is busy working out ways to make it easier for building owners to compile and report water consumption data. And just to make things more interesting, District members have recently committed to addressing stormwater management – an important environmental concern in Seattle – as part of its focus on water (Seattle 2030 District Strategic Plan 2014, 4). A stormwater calculator has been created to help with data collection (Combe August 17, 2015).

Combe feels there's significant untapped opportunity in small commercial buildings (under 50K square feet). "This is a massively underserved market. We are working with Lawrence Berkeley Laboratory (LBL) to guide a quick assessment process for District members in this category. We'll then provide some handholding and help them apply for incentives for simple improvements" (Combe August 17, 2015).

The 2030 District uses the Architecture 2030 Challenge for setting its performance goals. The Challenge recognizes that the built environment is the major source of global demand for energy and materials that produce by-product greenhouse gases (GHG). The ultimate goal is for the built environment to be carbon neutral by 2030. The Challenge also targets 50% reduction in emissions due to transportation by 2030, and a 50% reduction in water consumption by 2030.

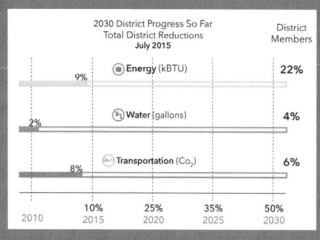

The illustration offers a snapshot as to how well the Seattle 2030 District is doing in regards to meeting Architecture 2030 Challenge performance goals. The bar chart shows the data for all buildings in the District area; the data for participating District members is represented at the right. As you can see, the building and water savings of those sharing their data within the District structure are nearly twice those when all buildings within the District boundaries are aggregated, using national averages for non-participating buildings. Although we are not privy to the reasons for non-participation, one can anticipate the peer pressure exerted by forward-thinking members of the 2030 District and the "business benefit" they receive from operational savings and marketing advantage in the Emerald City will convince non-participants to make improvements and join their competitors in this transformative partnership. One idea to encourage businesses (including current members) to increase participation in the District initiative, and in particular to share frankly about what's working and what's not, is to provide opportunities for the developer/owner/manager District members to meet in regular roundtables planned just for them. "They felt the larger stakeholder meetings often would just be opportunities for people trying to sell products and ideas," says Combe. 2030 District staff is in the process of scheduling these roundtable meetings in the coming year (Combe August 17, 2017).

The transformative value of this initiative goes well beyond Seattle's City limits. It has proved to be the model for several 2030 Districts throughout the U.S. Seattle has been joined by Cleveland, Pittsburgh, Denver, Stamford, San Francisco, Dallas, Toronto, Albuquerque, and Los Angeles. Today, over 230 square million square feet are committed to this effort. All of the 2030 District cities are linked through the 2030 District network, which works to "support peer exchange across Districts, store and share data, leverage the aggregate purchasing power of the District membership to secure reduced costs, create national partnership relationships, and influence national policy on transportation infrastructure and building water and energy efficiency" (2030 Districts, 2015).

Photo provided by JSH Properties.
Links to Project Information:
http://www.2030Districts.org/seattle/about
http://www.2030Districts.org/

Integration as a Change Management Process

Like others in the field, I believe that the most effective sustainable solutions, those that are restorative or regenerative and improve resilience, are achieved through an integrated approach. The EMERGE Leadership Model supports this approach and does this in a number of ways.

First, the model provides the proper focus for successful change intervention: mindset and process. Successful design processes, whether we are talking about designing and implementing a building project or product, a community, a policy, a program, or a curriculum, will prioritize mindset and process and utilize technology and tools appropriately.

Second, the model elicits leadership dispositions and skills that are important if integration is to be achieved. We've highlighted some of these in our earlier discussions of servant and aspirational leadership: systems thinking, foresight, witnessing, and constructive facilitation. We've highlighted others in our discussions of techniques you can use to develop the willingness to change, such as: shrinking the gap, providing meaning to the change, and persuasion.

Meanwhile, the process of integration, if done consciously and well, can act as the ideal container for creating the conditions for change required for the adoption of truly sustainable solutions. An integrated process can illuminate the tension between aspirations and the conventional approach to design. It can reveal the benefits and downsides of the specifics being considered. And it can be used to build confidence in achieving the aspired-to goals.

Within the context of the EMERGE Leadership Model, an integrated design process can act as a change management process. The most obvious change being managed is in the discovery of entirely new solutions – or innovative combinations of "tried and true" ideas – to the set of design conditions at hand. However, this result is really an artifact of a much more important evolution in the way the team is thinking about the problem.

This chapter discusses the practice of integration generally, and specifically as it is applied in designing sustainable solutions, both in its idealized form, and then as practitioners find ways to use it in the field. In the next chapter, Chapter 11, the practice of integration will be revisited in the context of collaboration – a major component of integration.

Not Prescribed, But Emergent

In their article "Time for Design" in *Rotman on Design*, Jeanne Liedtka and Henry Mintzberg, Professors of Business Administration and Management, discuss what they call a "conversational approach" in which the facilitator of a design process leads the conversation rather than produces the design. In their words, "the Community does the designing, and designers and users become almost indistinguishable" (Liedtka and Mintzberg 2013, 36). It is a highly collaborative process. The professors note: "Conversational design challenges leaders in ways that formulaic and visionary design do not.... Cultures that center on

hierarchy, expediency, and authoritarian leadership get in the way of good conversations." They add that "we all know about opportunities that exist in the white spaces...what we do not know is how to tap these opportunities" (Liedtka and Mintzberg 2013, 37). The authors suggest that conversational design is one way of accessing these opportunities. Conversation is only part of an integrated process. A thoughtfully constructed framework for design makes it safe to "see" and "see again." Creating a structure in which the parties are able and willing to look at things from multiple perspectives and at multiple points in time is critical to getting to the best solution possible.

Integration is the combining of elements into a whole, with the assumption that the sum will be greater than its parts. The integrated design process is a way to explore and implement design opportunities effectively on a project while staying within budgetary and scheduling constraints. Again, this process is not exclusive to green building design. It can be used in almost any type of design and/or decision-making process. Generally, it is a collaborative approach, not silo-based. It is an iterative process, with ongoing learning and emergent features. It is a flexible method using a comprehensible structure, but not a formula. And it is a process that is genuinely intended to find a solution that is not pre-determined.

Constraints such as the budget, the schedule, and existing conditions should inspire innovation, not shut it down. Professors Liedtka and Mintzberg recognize the dilemma of a process that is adaptive but not completely open-ended. In their words, "buildings have to be built, products brought to market, strategies implemented, and structures established," and the key "is to get the basics right so that the specifics can be easily changed" (Liedtka and Mintzberg 2013, 37).

The Idealized Process

7Group and Architect Bill Reed produced *The Integrative Design Guide to Green Building* to "redefine the practice of sustainability" (7 Group and Bill Reed, 2009). Their use of the term *integrative* is deliberate. It is intended to emphasize the fact that they are promoting an open, flexible process. Many in the field, including my colleagues at O'Brien & Company have taken their lead and have begun to use this term, and the acronym IP, for *integrative process*, to describe a collaborative process intended to create restorative solutions that do some good – and so in keeping with the dynamic model of sustainability presented in Chapter 3.

In their book, which they stress is *not* a cookbook, 7Group and Reed note that the process as they are presenting it is "idealized." "It will need to be adjusted and tailored to the parameters of each unique project and team" (7Group and Reed 2009, 101). In Figure 10.1 they compare the differences between

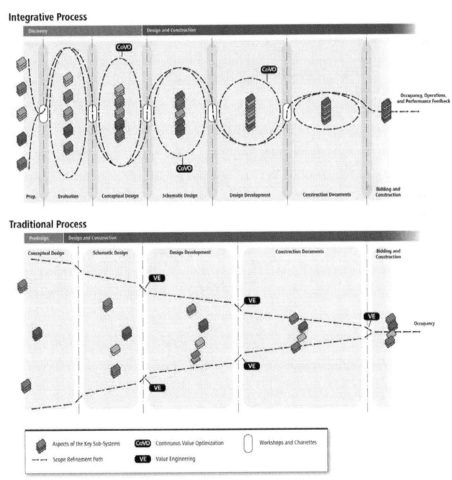

Figure 10.1: Image courtesy of 7group and Bill Reed, graphics by Corey Johnston

the idealized version(s) of "integrative process" and "traditional process."

The ability to achieve deep green, high performing buildings cost-effectively correlates directly with the quality of collaboration among project team members throughout design, construction, and early occupancy. The integrative process illustrated – however idealized – shows why. The process helps those involved to recognize how subsystems (habitat, water, energy, and materials) interrelate and to intentionally seek out synergies for better performance and more effective use of production resources (such as budget and labor). In the final analysis, the subsystems are closely aligned, working together to produce benefits that go far beyond brick and mortar. In his presentation at the first GreenBuild EuroMed in Italy (2015), Greg Kight of Jacobs used an "organic" model (See Figure 10.2) to discuss how applying the principles of integrative design benefitted the Intesa Sanpaolo Bank's Headquarters in Turin; the project was one of the first high rise towers to achieve LEED Platinum rating in Italy. Like the 7Group's illustration of integrative design, Kight's representation is an ideal to work toward (Kight 2015).

In the traditional, non-integrative process, the same subsystems exist, but the process does not leverage synergies. In a conventional construction project, contracts generally flow in a top-down manner,

Integrative Design - Building as Organism

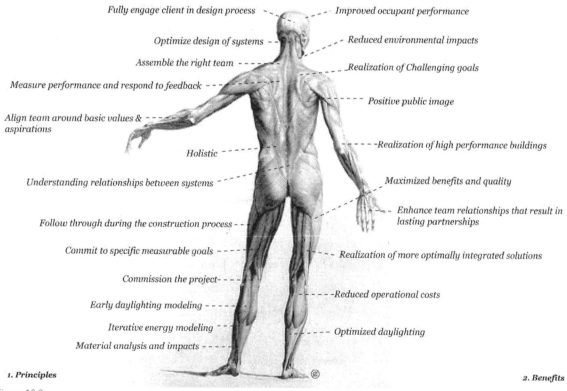

Fully engage client in design process
Optimize design of systems
Assemble the right team
Measure performance and respond to feedback
Align team around basic values & aspirations
Holistic
Understanding relationships between systems
Follow through during the construction process
Commit to specific measurable goals
Commission the project
Early daylighting modeling
Iterative energy modeling
Material analysis and impacts

Improved occupant performance
Reduced environmental impacts
Realization of Challenging goals
Positive public image
Realization of high performance buildings
Maximized benefits and quality
Enhance team relationships that result in lasting partnerships
Realization of more optimally integrated solutions
Reduced operational costs
Optimized daylighting

1. Principles

2. Benefits

Figure 10.2

with the owner contracting with the architect, and, separately, with the contractor, the general contractor contracting with subcontractors, and so on. The work is conducted in a linear fashion, with players brought into the process as their section of the work begins – and no sooner.

Design Industry Begins to Support Integration

Meaningful collaboration throughout design and construction provides opportunities for the project team to integrate building systems, which optimizes cost efficiencies and building performance, and reduces risk. For this reason, green building standards, such as LEED for Homes and Built Green have rewarded some level of integration in the design approach for some time. More recently, the U.S. Green Building Council piloted credits that reward the use of "integrative process" worksheets for specific project types and systems decisions. These credits are now included in LEED V.4 (USGBC, October 2014).

The ANSI IP Standard 2.0, successfully balloted in 2012, provides a common reference for all industry practitioners to help promote the use of IP. The idea is to optimize synergies among the systems (technical and living) associated with design and construction. Nora Daley-Peng represented O'Brien & Company on the team advising the ANSI IP Standard authors. It was our hope to contribute to a process that would help project teams realize meaningful cost savings, provide them with a deeper understanding of human and environmental interrelationships, and improve the environment for all living systems.

To support the implementation of integrated design

practice, the AIA developed a family of contracts under the title "Integrated Project Delivery" in 2008 (American Institute of Architects, 2015).

However, Bill Reed, co-author of the *Integrative Design Guide to Green Building* referenced earlier, and one of the authors of the ANSI IP Standard, cautions us: "[I]f sustainability goals are not part of the project, then IPD may earn you efficiencies in the process, but not necessarily sustainability" (Reed 6/11/13). This is a great example, by the way, where a tool (IPD contracts) will not necessarily provide you with the outcome you want if the collective mindset of the team, as reflected in project goals, is not aimed in that direction.

Ka-Ching, Ka-Ching

IP is sometimes understood as a series of meetings with lots of people talking about a problem. Despite the understanding that the process should allow for a better solution than any one of the individuals would on his or her own, it's easy to see why building owners and their representatives resist the idea. You can almost hear the "ka-ching, ka-ching!" resounding in their brains, as they assume costs will mount. O'Brien & Company's experience with integration led the company to take an approach that includes communication among everyone who should be involved, but which does not mean everyone has to be directly involved in every communication. Careful planning of meetings and agendas, as well as methods to incorporate "non-meeting" inputs, with an eye on moving the process along, is required.

Says Alistair Jackson, principal of O'Brien & Company: "While large group sessions are useful to get buy-in and alignment among a project's key stakeholders around goals and objectives, more focused work sessions with key team members can be very effective for identifying and critiquing strategies that will contribute to achieving those goals." To get the most value out of these more focused sessions, it will be important, says Jackson, "to make sure strategies being considered are critiqued from all perspectives; this helps identify barriers to implementation" (Jackson July 30, 2015). In addition to this critique function, it will be important to determine what research and analysis is needed, and the sequence, timing, and participation required to resolve issues the critique kicks up. The "pull planning" approach Elizabeth Powers discusses (see her essay: "Connecting the Dots") is one way to get this done. Jackson likes it because "it (pull planning) leverages commitment and accountability."

Especially with project teams that have committed to best practice, it can be useful to eliminate some of the more predictable measures from the conversation – for example, should there be bike racks or not? – and zero in on new, stickier issues. This prioritizing keeps the process focused on the value outcome and avoids redundancy. It also is a way to keep all team members engaged. Jackson cautions, however, not to "entirely eliminate opportunities to introduce new solutions even when the local industry has found a 'favorite' green technology, or to provide feedback on tried solutions that may not have worked well in a similar circumstance" (Jackson July 30, 2015).

Many project teams try to save money by communicating between large group sessions through email. Simply keeping stakeholders in the loop by putting them on an email distribution list doesn't actually achieve the intent of integrative process and comprehensive communication. One of the reasons that more regular large group sessions can have value: you are more likely to have everyone's attention than you might in an email. People do not tend to read their emails religiously, especially when the emails resemble opuses. As in so many things, when it comes to communicating between meetings with email, "less is more." Jackson suggests limiting your team email communications to three priority items. He says, "If 50% of your team grasps those three items, this is substantially better than when only 5% of the team reads a more comprehensive email. You don't have to (and shouldn't try to) cover everything. If your team is engaged and interested they will likely come back with questions about things they don't see in the message" (Jackson July 30, 2015).

Note that in the idealized integrative process (refer back to Figure 10.1), the final stage doesn't conclude at turnover from construction to occupancy. Rather, it includes the operational phase, and performance feedback loops both internally, and to future projects. Effective communication must be maintained not only within each phase but also across the transition between phases. However well integrated the process is, the transition from construction to occupancy often brings new people to the table who have not fully bought into the vision.

Skillful project communications can help avoid unnecessary expense, and that is true whether the team takes an integrative process approach or a traditional one. The difference with IP is that it allows more opportunities to communicate, and it recognizes that *the earlier team members are brought into the*

Connecting the Dots

By Elizabeth A.D. Powers, LEED AP BD+C, ID+C

We've all seen diagrams of the idealized process of integrative design. Frequently they show large nodes or "dots" for all-team meetings, with little "dots" in between representing interim milestones (which may be meetings or other work). For those large dots to represent true progress – and effective integration – the interim work must be done, and be done well. To make integrative design effective in practice, we need effective ways to connect the dots. One method which seems particularly helpful is *pull planning*. In contrast to critical path scheduling, where activities, durations, and related tasks are identified and an end date calculated, pull planning starts with the end in mind. According to the Lean Construction Institute: "A pull plan is a plan for executing a specific phase of a project using a pull technique to determine hand-offs. It is prepared by the team actually responsible for doing the work through conversation. Work is planned at the 'request' of a downstream 'customer'" (Lean Construction Institute July 15, 2015).

An example might be this: the project team comes out of an eco-charrette in the concept design phase – a large dot – with high level goals and some criteria around energy performance. But a specific EUI (Energy Use Index) target has not been set. However, the next time the whole team meets (the next large dot), they need to have one or two primary system types identified. An integrative process would require understanding the optimum energy requirement – the EUI target – in order to do the latter. With pull planning, the project team works backwards, figuring out what they need to know and by when, to determine how the goals might translate to an EUI, in order to select systems that will meet them. Working backwards, they will identify little dots or milestones to help them achieve this. In this example, setting an EUI (Energy Use Index) target could involve meeting with future building managers, researching similar building types, looking at local code pathways (especially alternates that allow more flexibility if higher performance is reached), or translating organizational commitments to lowering greenhouse gas footprints down to the building level.

My colleague Alistair Jackson stresses the importance of identifying the underlying "value" in pull planning (or similar processes): "Understanding what the true 'value' is to the downstream customer helps you more precisely identify the important steps in the value chain. It also helps you identify (and eliminate) steps that don't add or preserve value, finally helping you determine the flow and hand-offs to deliver the *best* value. The 'value' of an end result can vary from project to project but should be explicitly understood by the project team. This highlights the importance of goal and objective setting in IP. Those things define value for the project stakeholders. Without clear articulation of 'values' it is virtually impossible to define the value chain" (Jackson July 30, 2015).

One of the benefits of using pull planning (also

Connecting the Dots (Continued)

known as "phase" planning) is that it is part of Lean, a process already accepted in the industry, to actualize integrative design, delivery, and operation. It's a way to psychologically "shrink the gap" (something suggested by the Heaths in *Switch* and discussed in Chapter 9) by using a familiar tool to accomplish something new. Within the context of pull planning, the emergent leader in the facilitator role can help a team discover what needs to be done to achieve sustainable building goals, by whom, and when to get the key decisions for that point in the process made, and made right. ✒

dialogue the better.

Teams involved in an integrated design process develop a shared vision that they can refer back to as the process unfolds. According to Wheatley, this act of "self-reference" is "key to facilitating orderly change in the midst of turbulent environments" (Wheatley 2006, 86). It's also what happens in fractals. They continually refer back to the same equation and beautiful patterns emerge, just at different scales (see Figure 10.3). In a truly open, collaborative process, individuals bring their logical and intuitive selves to the table. Because there is a constant upon which everyone agrees early on, and a commitment to work effectively to develop a shared understanding of the project resulting from that earlier vision, the process is safe for all participants – and the result will be uniquely appropriate and quite beautiful!

Long-time colleague and author Ann Edminster discusses how the process of developing and delivering a shared vision can actually save money

in her essay, "Priceless Outcomes from an Integrated Approach." Number-crunchers should be calling for IP, not discouraging it. Alistair Jackson notes, "it might surprise that the [U.S.] federal government is calling for many aspects of IP in their model Design Build process; in some cases even opening the discussion to higher first costs in order to enhance savings down the road due to greater resilience and energy performance" (Jackson August 11, 2015).

Good meeting planning is a critically important skill for anyone leading an integrated design or collaborative process. In Chapter 11, we'll discuss the collaborative process in the context of emergent leadership. In Chapter 12 we'll offer some tips on designing meetings.

Figure 10.3

Priceless Outcomes from an Integrated Approach

By Ann V. Edminster, M. Arch

There are many ways of illustrating an integrated/integrative process, but my favorite is a pair of graphs developed by attorney Will Lichtig (Boldt Company), shown below.

These graphs depict common understanding developing over time as the design and construction process unfolds. In a traditional (sequential, siloed) project, common understanding develops rather slowly, as various parties join the project team by stages. Shared understanding only begins to increase significantly once construction has begun, and finally reaches its peak at the job's conclusion. Decidedly sub-optimal.

By contrast, when an integrated design and delivery approach is taken, all principals join the project team very early in the process, and as a result common understanding rises very quickly, reaching a peak long before construction starts. "Notable among the numerous benefits of this early, heightened degree of understanding are greatly increased opportunities to identify synergies and avoid system conflicts. These in turn improve the project across many dimensions of performance; reduce mistakes, oversights, and change orders; and thus can yield significant cost savings."

Somewhat less obvious are the myriad corollary benefits, including the team's greater investment in the goal outcomes, stronger cohesion and shared sense of purpose, reduced likelihood of developing adversarial relationships, increased productivity and work satisfaction, and overall happiness and harmony among the players. With these yields from an integrative approach, it's virtually impossible not to do better work, both individually and collectively.

Note: Integrated Design and Delivery is a term coined by a team of integrated design and integrated project delivery practitioners working on a guide to integrative processes for the Commission for Environmental Cooperation's Green Building Construction Task Force in June 2014. (Ann Edminster is task force chair.)

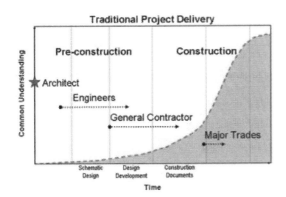

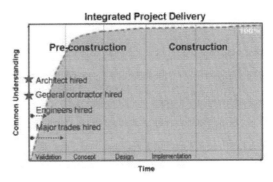

What is Emergent Collaboration?

In the Emerge Leadership Model, the third component is Community. (Figure 11.1) The foundation for this component is collaboration. Merriam-Webster defines collaboration as "[working] jointly with others or together especially in an intellectual endeavor" (merriam- webster. com/dictionary/collaborate). Ideally, collaboration is not just the act of working together to achieve a defined "intellectual endeavor," but also a way of working together that produces long- term relationships and the capacity and will to continue working together in a positive manner. It is a mindful process that goes far beyond what often passes for collaboration today – collecting ideas on a flip chart (physical or virtual) or via colorful post-its, transcribing the results into a draft report and/or design, allowing for comments on the report and/or design, integrating those comments (and this is not guaranteed), and calling it sufficient.

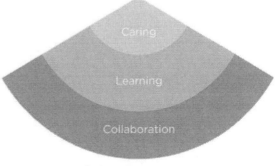

COMMUNITY

Figure 11.1

Healthy collaboration is inclusive: it starts with the basic assumption that *everyone* in the room has something significant to *contribute.*

At the same time, it recognizes that *everyone* in the room has something to *learn*. Healthy collaboration is structured so that all participants truly see and care for each other as persons.

So, what is *emergent* collaboration? Remember that emergent leadership, as we have defined it, has a specific goal in mind: to accelerate the implementation of life-sustaining solutions in the built environment. And also remember that this approach represents a dramatic change from the norm. The collaboration we are envisioning is not about a group of individuals coming together to agree on just any idea. And remember further that the first and most important place to intervene in a system is at the mindset level. The second is process. With emergent collaboration, we address mindset and we create a change management process that is intended to foster change.

An emergent leader facilitating a collaborative process must analyze and account for attitudes toward an envisioned change. An effective emergent leader will ask: Where are participating individuals and/or organizations on the spectrum of willingness to change toward the larger vision of sustainability? As the collaboration proceeds and the vision is clarified and defined for this particular group or team, what attitudes toward the larger vision, or aspects of the vision, reveal themselves?

Further, an emergent leader applies principles from positive psychology by creating opportunities for joyful, shared learning throughout the collaborative process. The openness created in an optimistic atmosphere is much more likely to elicit new thinking

and new behaviors. I have seen this work in the development of green building programs, where contractors got so excited about a new idea for a wall assembly they actually forgot they were competitors. Of course, everybody won in that situation! No doubt you have been to a collaborative session where the learning consisted of a lecture/presentation by an "expert" with Q&A thrown in, if time allowed? Not ideal.

And finally, an emergent leader will be looking for explicit opportunities to foster and grow servant leadership within the collaborating group, certainly through modeling, and hopefully through mentoring. Ideally, and especially if the emergent leader facilitating the collaboration is an outside consultant to the group, it will be important to look for opportunities to encourage servant leaders within the group to consider the practice of emergence.

In summary, emergent leadership enhances collaboration by:

- Analyzing and accounting for attitudes toward an envisioned change – it addresses mindset!
- Explicitly incorporating joyful, shared learning.
- Proactively identifying and growing leaders.

Why is Emergent Collaboration So Important?

The first reason should be obvious: The process leads to solutions that are grounded in where the participants are coming from, what they know, and what they learn through it. Thus, the solutions are more likely to be implemented from a genuine, rooted place. This is more than buy-in or even ownership; it is stewardship of the highest order. Second, like the

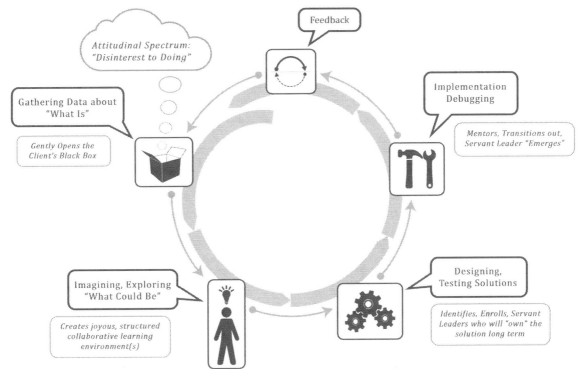

Feedback

Implementation
Debugging

*Mentors, Transitions out,
Servant Leader "Emerges"*

*Attitudinal Spectrum:
"Disinterest to Doing"*

Gathering Data about
"What Is"

*Gently Opens the
Client's Black Box*

Designing,
Testing Solutions

*Identifies, Enrolls, Servant
Leaders who will "own" the
solution long term*

Imagining, Exploring
"What Could Be"

*Creates joyous, structured
collaborative learning
environment(s)*

Figure 11.2

integrative design process, an emergent collaboration is intended to foster creativity, and thus is more likely to lead to restorative, "living" solutions. Third, the process of emergent collaboration develops leaders who can foster and encourage long-term and effective implementation of the solutions that emanate from the process. And, fourth, the process builds caring communities, which leads to further willingness to ask hard questions, listen, and grow together – fostering "living" solutions that transform beyond "bricks and mortar."

What Does This Emergent Collaboration Look Like?

In Figure 11.2, the open-ended spiral shape is intended to imply a process that is iterative. For simplicity's sake, however, we are portraying just one cycle. This

schematic is an outcome of a "whiteboard" exercise during the RBUFW Project (see "Transformation in Practice: Rainier Beach Urban Farm & Wetlands," earlier), and as in that project, our schematic assumes the emergent leader is an "outside consultant" who will eventually depart from the community. The red (dark) icons and labels are steps that most consultants should recognize. The grey (light) labels provide extra guidance to those facilitating emergent collaboration.

What Is: (Figure 11.3) In the first step of the schematic, the emergent leader/consultant performs discovery – looking at what is or what conditions exist. In many design and building projects, this research is about the physical conditions an existing or proposed site offers, ecological health, land use, structural integrity. It often also includes gathering data about existing

Attitudinal Spectrum:
"Disinterest to Doing"

Gathering Data about
"What Is"

Gently Opens the
Client's Black Box

Figure 11.3

(and frequently long-standing) desires related to the project, as well as the financial and policy picture. This step often reveals "constraints." (I recall a consultant listing an aerie on a proposed site as a "constraint" to be mitigated. I generally urge participants to see "constraints" as opportunities to be creative.)

One of the most skillful examples of discovery behavior is Art Castle. I met Art in the mid-90's when Kitsap County and the Kitsap HomeBuilders Association (KHBA) were considering putting together a voluntary green building program. The program would be called Build a Better Kitsap, later renamed Built Green Kitsap, and would be the first green building program in Washington State, the second in the country. Art was the Executive Director for the KHBA, an organization that in the early '90s had rebuffed my efforts to meet with when I was planning the Building with Val-

ue Conference in 1993. I found Art receptive, however. He saw the opportunity to work with Kitsap County as a win-win-win with the industry leading rather than being led. And he practiced the art of discovery as naturally as drinking water. For him, it was all about building relationships.

On this and every project thereafter that I was a party to, by the time Art gathered people into a room, he'd already forged a relationship with each and every individual who could benefit and contribute to the project's success. On the phone, over lunch at a diner (he likes salty fries), or at a sidebar during a community meeting, Art would chat people up, learning what they cared about, and providing information about how he thought the program might fulfill a need they were expressing. This "discovery" process would mean that by the time people came together, his work

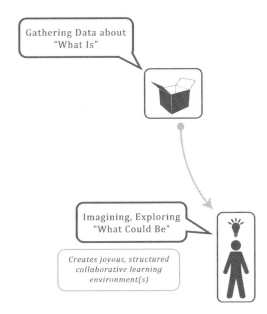

Gathering Data about "What Is"

Imagining, Exploring "What Could Be"

Creates joyous, structured collaborative learning environment(s)

Figure 11.4

was halfway done! He and I would plan collaborative meetings with this information in hand, and it made all the difference.

In the last project I consulted on with Art, our task was to create a <u>set of guidelines for Low Impact Development</u> (LID) in Kitsap County. We led a multi-disciplinary team with specific and relevant technical expertise. Our working committee, which also brought technical skills to the table, had representatives from industry and government from all four local cities and the County. Art's initial groundwork identifying the right players and understanding what they cared about went a long way toward the result that for the first time ever, when the resulting guidance document was completed, it was adopted unanimously by all of the jurisdictions involved.

With emergent collaboration, I recommend research-ing attitudes about sustainable solutions that might apply to the project and plotting these graphically, i.e. in a "quick and dirty" sketch. This helps us "see" how the individual parties to the discussion feel about those ideas, and where the group stands as a whole. The discovery process can also identify those items that are already favored (which may or may not be the "best possible" opportunity). Such research can illuminate what might be necessary psychologically to "shrink the gap" between established thinking and innovative re-thinking. *Witnessing*, which we have al-ready discussed, is an important attribute of the emer-gent leader and is a skill that comes in handy here. Attitudes aren't wrong, they simply *are*.

What Could Be: (Figure 11.4) The next step in the spiral is to imagine and explore what could be. As

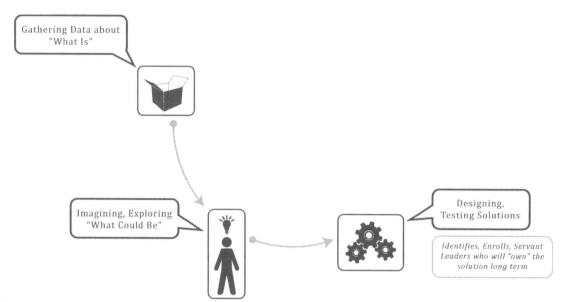

Figure 11.5

noted in grey, the emergent distinction is that as part of this process, joyous, shared learning is structured into the thinking process. I incorporate adult learning principles into planning collaborative meetings. For example, adults like to learn something they can apply immediately in their personal and/or professional life.

During the exploration phase of the LID Guidelines Project, each monthly meeting included a public workshop in the morning on topics the working committee had identified as important if they were to knowledgeably develop the guidelines. Sometimes members of our technical consultant team delivered the education, but more often the presenters were peers from other parts of the Puget Sound region with hands-on experience with the best management practice we were exploring. The committee then rolled

up their sleeves in an afternoon working session to use what they'd learned that morning in free-ranging discussions of what could be, covering the walls and tables with marked up flip charts, color coded post-its, and quickly drawn sketches.

Testing: (Figure 11.5) The next step in the spiral is to test the design or solutions that were envisioned in "what could be" activities. In the LID project, this meant taking the guidelines the consultants had compiled using the decisions made by the working committee, as well the body of technical expertise the committee represented, and "reviewing" how they would impact development in the participating jurisdictions. These guidelines were also reviewed to see whether they would indeed have a positive influence on the environment, and what practical implications would

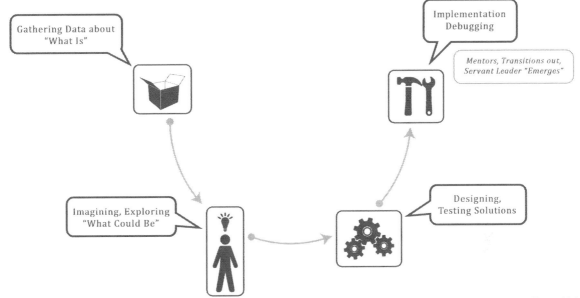

Figure 11.6

result. Since the working committee members were knee deep in this review process, they were also engaged in learning, and invested as a result.

Testing reveals concerns or better future possibilities. Testing can also validate intuitive hunches that arose in earlier conversations. During this phase especially, it was important when the committee came together for review sessions that the facilitators (myself and Alistair Jackson of O'Brien & Company) practice constructive facilitation: questioning, synthesizing, and contributing. By doing so, we could avoid getting lost in the weeds, and maintain momentum. If not before this point, the emergent leader should be identifying, enrolling, and mentoring servant leaders who will own the project's solutions long term. In the LID project example, Art was stimulating leadership

right from the beginning.

Debugging: (Figure 11.6) In implementation, "bugs" will inevitably reveal themselves. It will be important to continue to see this step as a "learning exercise." Modeling a humble frame of mind and keeping a sense of humor is an important aspect of this step. Outside consultants are often being phased out at this point in most projects, especially those with public funding. In our ideal spiral, however, we suggest the consultant use this opportunity to mentor emergent leadership in servant leaders who you have identified in the previous step. This is a critical moment in the process, and often momentum is lost here.

In the LID example, finalizing the guidelines deliverable (a key component of implementation, but

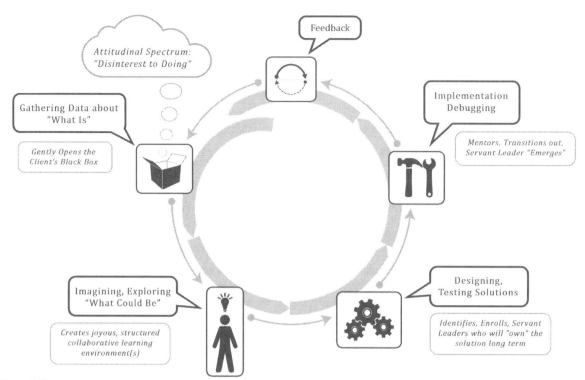

Feedback

Attitudinal Spectrum:
"Disinterest to Doing"

Gathering Data about
"What Is"

Gently Opens the
Client's Black Box

Implementation
Debugging

Mentors, Transitions out,
Servant Leader "Emerges"

Imagining, Exploring
"What Could Be"

Creates joyous, structured
collaborative learning
environment(s)

Designing,
Testing Solutions

Identifies, Enrolls, Servant
Leaders who will "own" the
solution long term

Figure 11.7

one which did not engage the working committee) took longer than hoped, largely due to some unforeseen and unfortunate personnel changes on the technical consulting team. Luckily for the project, and for us, Art had stored a lot of good will with the project stakeholders, and as mentioned above, the final deliverable was adopted unanimously by all of the jurisdictions involved.

Feedback: (Figure 11.7) At the "conclusion" of the cycle, feedback is critical for success, yet it is seldom sought in a meaningful manner for a variety of reasons, not the least of which is personal investment by funders or consultant. Again, humility and a sense of humor are important here. In an ideal situation, feedback provides input into the next generation of the given work-product or idea. And in an ideal situation, there is appetite and space for utilizing that input.

Emergent collaboration calls for a much more open and adaptive view of the process we use to do our work. The closer we move towards this ideal, the more likely we will achieve truly sustainable solutions.

I've employed an example of using an emergent collaborative process to develop policy. In his essay describing the integrative design process, Bill Reed, Founder of Regenesis provides an example of applying similar principles to a design project.

The Integrative Design Process – a Process to Develop Will

By Bill Reed, AIA, LEED AP

"The future is not just about firefighting and tinkering with the surface of structural change. It's not just about replacing one mindset that no longer serves us with another.... It's a future that requires us to tap into a deeper level of humanity, of who we really are and who we want to be as a society. It is a future that we can sense, feel, and actualize by shifting the inner place from which we operate.... This inner shift...is at the core of all deep leadership work today. It's a shift that requires us to expand our thinking from the head to the heart. It is a shift from an ego-system awareness that cares about the well-being of oneself to an eco-system awareness that cares about the well-being of all, including oneself.... When operating with eco-system awareness we are driven by concerns and intentions of our emerging and essential self – that is, by a concern that is informed by the well-being of the whole" (Scharmer & Kaufer 2013, 1).

When we ask design teams and workshop participants to identify the significant barriers to achieving a sustainable condition, the answers range from various technical to social perspectives: we need new technologies, more money, new economic systems, new values embedded in a culture, and so on. All are valid, of course. Yet, there is one foundational dimension of developing human achievement that is rarely considered: *Will*.

The most significant barrier standing in the way of achieving an integrated and healthy relationship with life on this planet is the lack of the will to do so.

Included in the domain of will is the willingness to be deeply curious and introspective. For, of course, will without understanding, has no direction. If we could intentionally develop will in ourselves, our organizations and teams, we have the potential to rapidly shift our behaviors and focus to do what it takes to achieve a sustainable condition. After all, this issue is really not a technology or money problem; we, as humans, have lived appropriately and successfully in a co-evolutionary state with life on this planet in the past. All the technologies needed to live sustainably exist right now. Lack of political will, the will of groupthink, the self-centered will of each of us as individuals stand in the way of achieving the significant actions and states-of-being that are needed for humans and nature to thrive together.

For example, lack of money is often used for the reason to not engage in higher levels of achievement, no matter if the subject is a green building, infrastructure maintenance, or level of education. But money is rarely an issue; after all it is only a social construct. Personal example: I had a girlfriend on the other side of the continent when I was in college. I had no money, yet I made the cross-country trip quite a few times using my thumb, sharing rides, and delivering cars. Another example, with no money, the U.S. found the resources to fund its role in World War II. It did the seemingly impossible and sent a man to the moon within 10 years. And we know the highest performing green buildings are built for equal and

The Integrative Design Process – a Process to Develop Will (Continued)

lower capital cost than a conventional budget. Yet there is always someone or groupthink that says it can't be done – and we let those without will or understanding – the "realists" – drag us down.

Will is the source of energy that drives us to excel beyond expectations and the norm. With *will* as a driver, the possibilities are open and endless.

How do we consciously awaken will to engage the mental and emotional states that become even more powerful and effective when engaged as an aligned group?

There are a number of mental frameworks that can help structure the development of will and the practice to sustain it through the course of a project, a business, or a even a community and its ecology. These frameworks have been around for hundreds, if not thousands of years.

Here are four ways for framing human activity. These come from a number of traditions and sources:

- What, How, Why
- Hand, Heart, Mind
- Body, Mind, Spirit
- Function, Being, Will

These dimensions are present in every interaction between two or three people. They are present in every meeting and in each one of us.

For an example of how this can be useful, let's use "function, being, and will" as framing for creating a family dinner.

1. Function: Prep and cook the food;
2. Being: Sit down and serve the food in a way that we share our love and/or our daily activities with each other;
3. Will: So that our children have the nourishment and psychological well-being to grow into responsible adults.

This third element is the why or the deeper purpose of the activity. The *will* is what motivates us to actually take the time to cook the meal and sit down for an hour with the family. If we didn't have the will to support the development of our children, we could just as easily have bought a bag of burgers, thrown it at the kids, and sent them to the TV room while we downed a few beers. The will is what gives direction and impetus to the ultimate outcome.

An example from the world of building: We were recently engaged in facilitating an integrative design process for a large wastewater treatment plant. Money was seen as the primary driver along with references to general sustainability goals and community involvement. By taking the time to align the very large team and the multiple communities around the higher potential of this facility, and what it could mean to the communities it served, the project shifted from being simply a

slightly less ugly and less smelly sewage plant to something meaningful in many dimensions.

How did we "awaken" the will required to make this shift? 7Group and I have written extensively about the integrative process in our book, *The Integrative Design Guide to Green Building: Redefining the Practice of Sustainability*. One very important ingredient in the awakening process is asking questions that shift the team's thinking to the purpose and effect of the project on the larger community and ecological system. A couple of examples of these questions: What might be the beneficial effect this project could have on the watershed and the cultural systems in this place? What relationships need to be developed in order to understand what would be most meaningful for life in this community, as well as reciprocally beneficial for the effectiveness of this treatment plant? As a result of exploring "What healthy interrelationships could this project catalyze?" rather than "How can we make this wastewater facility better?" we ended up with a vision that was very energizing. The community and the design team looked at how the project could conceptually become a freshwater processing facility, an integrated resource for heat and nutrients, a resource center that served as a community meeting place, a place that demonstrated the business of the water cycle, a park, and a generative asset for long-term sustainability development.

In addition to creating greater alignment – and willingness to contribute financially to the project on the part of local towns – this "purposeful" conversation, which took an "additional" four months on the project's timeline, actually decreased the design time by six months. The project was unanimously approved, and the permit was granted 18 months faster than originally anticipated.

Giving people the chance to imagine a future that is meaningful and important to them, going beyond the usual and the expected, and inspiring individuals and groups to discover new ideas and possibilities, all these can be *the most practical* aspect of engaging our efforts in the reach towards sustainability.

Joyful Learning Is Key to Leadership Within Community

In Chapter 10, I asserted that healthy collaboration recognizes that everyone in the room has something to learn. Further, I noted that with emergent collaboration, shared, joyous learning is explicitly structured into the thinking process. Why is learning – and especially shared, joyous learning – so important to effective leadership within the context of community?

Fostering the Willingness to Learn Through Play

Let's start with learning. An emergent leader seeks to create an atmosphere where learning is not only allowed but fostered; it engenders *teachability* – that is, the willingness to learn. This willingness to learn is absolutely critical to innovation. Participants in collaborative ventures who are willing to learn (or even willing to be willing to learn) are much more likely to consider something they didn't "know" or "believe" before. In fact, they may be willing to "change their minds!"

This openness to new ideas is even greater when the process offers a level playing field to all participants. In such situations, expertise is provided by *all* those participating in a collaborative problem-solving process. For outside consultants who may be applying the principles of emergent leadership, it will be especially important to honor and elicit the indigenous intelligence offered by the client community. (David Eisenberg calls this "in-pertise.")

Further, if the proposal to learn occurs within the context of *play*, we enhance this openness. According to Dr. Stuart Brown (Brown and Vaughn 2009, 43), there is evidence that "with enough play, the brain works better. We feel more optimistic and more creative." Brown, who bases his theories on studies of animals in the lab and in nature, the scientific observation of humans at play, and play histories he has collected from hundreds of clients, concludes that when we tap into the genius of play, "we open ourselves to creating imaginative, new cognitive combinations" (Brown and Vaughn 2009, 37). Play helps us find new ways to solve problems – and isn't that just what we need? In addition, behavioral science reveals that play fosters social cohesion, which is especially important when developing solutions where deeply felt differences or long-held views are at work. For adults, says Brown, play is a way to "put us in sync with those around us...a way to tap into common emotions" (Brown and Vaughn 2009, 63).

Have you ever attended a public meeting where a strongly negative viewpoint drowns out any other view? Emotions are contagious. So, it's important – even when opinions differ - to create an environment where the emotional atmosphere is positive and open. Play, or even simply holding a playful attitude, helps foster that positive environment.

Playful Contexts Create Better Solutions

Playfulness doesn't just keep us from beating each other up. It helps us solve problems more creatively. "The genius of play is that, in playing, we create imaginative new cognitive combinations. And in creating those novel combinations, we find what works" (Brown and Vaughn 2009, 37).

Brown emphasizes that "play is a state of mind" rather than an activity. An angry round of golf may be a "game," but is not playful. Brown defines play as "an absorbing, apparently purposeless activity that provides enjoyment and a suspension of self-consciousness and sense of time" (Brown and Vaughn 2009, 60). It's enjoyable enough that you want to repeat or continue the experience.

In a 2008 TED Talk on Creativity and Play, Tim Brown (CEO of IDEO, no relation to Stuart), agrees that playfulness helps us get to "better, creative solutions." In his talk, Tim Brown describes three forms of play that adults can use to generate great ideas in a team setting: exploratory play (brainstorming, where quantity not quality is the goal, and even the ridiculous is okay); construction play (where you make things with your hands); and role play (where you can walk through the experience of solutions you are envisioning). Elements of generative (divergent) thinking and solution development (convergent thinking) – key aspects of integrative design – can be seen in each of these play formats.

Tim Brown believes we need trust in order to play and to be creative. To "make play work" in adult settings, it's important that the players agree on the rules, and on when and how to play. An important aspect of any collaborative effort, and especially when you're hoping participants feel trusting enough to play, is creating a safe "container" for participants. It seems like an oxymoron: to foster creativity through a sense of safety. And yet, as Tim Brown noted in his talk, "Fear is the root of our conservatism" (Brown, 2008).

It Takes Work to Create Playful Contexts

It might seem tedious to spend time carefully thinking through a collaborative session. But it is absolutely necessary to creating a positive environment, one in which joyous learning (and creative problem solving) will be the result. Regardless of whether your envisioned play is as simple as a round of brainstorming, or a complex role-play scenario, participants need to be provisioned with supplies, time, and clear directions, so that they ask themselves, "Why not [play]?" (As opposed to declaring, "I'd rather not!")

Of course, it is important, too, to make clear "Why [we are doing this playing]." This returns us to Chapter 10, where we describe the earliest stage of an emergent collaborative initiative as "discovery" – conducting research among the participants about their concerns, potential contributions and attitudes toward the problem at hand. There should be a direct line between the "why" of the meeting and the concerns and potential contributions of the participants. If not, why are they there? They'd like to know.

Setting the Stage for Openness and Play

One of the exercises we've created to open the EMERGE Leadership workshop is designed to create a safe space for sharing and learning in the moment, while demonstrating an easy way to open a meeting creatively without being accomplished artists.

Before the workshop begins, we prepare a large sheet of butcher or kraft paper as follows: we create a "hopes" section along the top of the chart (signaled by a thriving tree), and a much larger "concerns" section along the bottom of the chart, (signaled by the roots

of the tree. We populate the concerns section with "star people" outlines in a variety of colors – enough for everyone attending, including faculty. When participants first enter the room, we invite them to claim one of the outlines (encouraging them to gravitate to a color they like) and write their name as well as a "role" or personality they are showing up as.

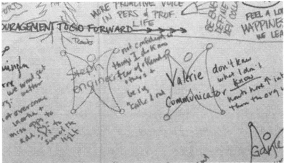

Figure 12.1

Figure 12.2

Figures 12.1 and 12.2 are workshop photos taken by former City of Portland Green Team Manager (and emergent leader himself) Mike O'Brien during the process conducted at the Portland-based Earth Advantage Headquarters. From Figure 12.1 you can see that one participant chose to identify as "communicator," another as "engineer." Others identified as "resourceful," "manager," and "listener." The star people and tree drawing are simple and easy to replicate.

As part of this initial and *individual* exercise, we then ask our participants to reflect quietly to themselves on their hopes and concerns regarding the workshop.

We follow with roundrobin introductions during which we ask participants to share briefly with the group their hopes and concerns. As shown in Figure 12.2, we record these on the charts as well, noting the concerns by their chosen "star person" outline in the roots section of the chart. We record their hopes in the upper "tree" section, generally trying to include a symbol or a very concise phrase to signify the latter. (We don't shy from using humorous symbols or phrases when they are called for!) We use two recorders to maintain momentum. (That's Ann Edminster in the photo.) The exercise doesn't take any longer than the traditional round-robin introductions might; in fact sometimes it's shorter. And it often includes laughter as well as some serious moments. This two-step process (from individual to group activity) helps integrate the less extroverted into the mix.

While we routinely conduct a pre-workshop survey to collect information from individuals coming to the workshop, including such things as their hopes and concerns, only the faculty is privy to this confidential information. By the time the "star people" exercise is complete, however, we are all on the same page. The connection in the room is palpable.

We then post the charts where they can be seen and re-visited from time to time. The colorful charts are visual reminders for everyone of their personal "Why?" and serve as a gentle reminder to everyone in the room of what their fellow participants are bringing to the workshop experience. During the closing session we use the charts to check in. Have our hopes and fears have been addressed satisfactorily? So far, this exercise has worked flawlessly.

Design Principles for Meetings

In addition to taking the time upfront to prepare for a collaborative session, and above all making sure there is alignment between the purpose of the session and the participants who attend, there are a few meeting design principles that the emergent leader should keep in mind. I am grateful to my colleagues Kelly Lerner and Alli Kingfisher for sharing these essentials at EMERGE Workshops and Living Future educational events; they can make meetings more productive:

- Invite everyone's voice in the room to be heard early on.
- Provide a rhythm that balances the energy of play and reflection, divergent and convergent thinking, individual, small group, and large group activities.
- Balance processes to allow both introverts and extroverts (high-power/low-power) to contribute, and harvest the expertise of everyone in the room.
- Treat all contributions as equally significant, and all participants as equally deserving of respect.

The most important thing is to be genuine (and serious) about your invitation to contribute. Brainstorming ground rules at the outset can be a good idea, but only if you actually follow them.

The emergent leader, whether the facilitator or not, can model behavior that aligns with these meeting design principles. As a facilitator, an emergent leader might "poll" participants, rather than allowing the vocal (and likely extroverted) participant(s) to dominate the conversation. As a participant, an emergent leader might really listen, and thoughtfully contribute to the dialogue, rather than monopolize it. In addition, the emergent leader-participant might model a positive attitude towards suggestions to "try on" something new or to play. (See Sidebar: "What Meeting Planners Need to Know" for more advice on planning meetings effectively, pages 111-112.)

Easy Does It, But Do It

Stuart Brown believes that "joy is our birthright, and is intrinsic to our essential design [as humans]" (Brown and Vaughn 2009, 147). He also says play at work is not just useful, but *essential*. "Work does not work without play" (Brown and Vaughn 2009, 129). Not just a good idea, but essential! Brown works with highly competitive, serious people who, when they realized they have missed joy in their lives because of an inability to play, are seriously unhappy. As emergent leaders we are sure to run into serious professionals who believe play is a "waste" of time. (Maybe, dear reader, you are one of them.)

Brown advises gentleness when introducing adults to play in a professional setting. He suggests, with emphasis, that, "...*movement* of any sort – has a way of getting past our mental defenses" (Brown and Vaughn 2009, 150). Play doesn't necessarily have to look like a game of "Twister." Earlier in the discussion of "liking" in Chapter 9, I mentioned scheduling a site walk prior to the sit-down meeting. Folks who wouldn't necessarily interact get to, and they generally have lots of fun doing it. (Especially if you treat it as a game.

For example, assigning them to find things on the site, and racking up points if they do.)

In *Transformative Scenario Planning*, Adam Kahane talks about the healing power of a one-hour walk assigned to participants in the "Vision Guatemala" project. Team members were to choose a walking partner who they felt was most different from them. Kahane reports that, upon return, some participants were "literally staggering from the astonishment of having seen their common context through such different eyes" (Kahane 2013, 39). It's likely that the shared physical aspect (i.e., the participants' movement) of this exercise was as important as the topics they covered.

Using Scenarios to Create New Possibilities

Earlier in the book I discussed the importance of prioritizing mindset and process over tools and technology. That said, tools and technology can be properly used to enhance process and trigger re-thinking (thus opening the mind to new possibilities). One tool we make good use of in the EMERGE Leadership workshop is a team planning exercise that utilizes scenarios to address leadership challenges that members of the group are actually facing or could face.

Prior to the workshop, we survey participants for situations they are dealing with and would be willing to address in a team setting. Elements of these situations are integrated into a scenario template I've developed. Several scenarios are developed, and participants self-select the scenario they want to work on and together form a self-directed team. The team spends at least two hours working on the scenario (more if they want to), another hour or so preparing a presentation of both the results and reporting on their team process, and twenty minutes to present. We provide lots of arts and crafts supplies to make this fun – and therefore more memorable! Figure 12.3 shows one team working on their project in the living room of the Islandwood guest lodge after dinner.

Figure 12.3

Many groups decide to move beyond typical presentation styles when presenting their results to the group. Figure 12.4 shows one group's illustrated flip-chart book created to introduce their team presentation. Figure 12.5 shows a team demonstrating "Ready, Fire, Aim," a funny, misguided, but unfortunately too common way to implement change.

Figure 12.4

The team planning segment of the workshop is an opportunity for everyone to practice some of the ideas presented in the workshop while applying them to realistic leadership situations. The presentation segment helps the team figure out how to communicate what they've done and learned. Once the presentation is complete, the group receives constructive comments from faculty and the group at large (see Figure 12.6). During this discussion, we touch in particular on how the solution to the challenge addressed by the group reflects the EMERGE Leadership approach vs. conventional leadership approaches.

Figure 12.5

The leadership issue of concern can be a personal one, such as "I'm concerned about how my attempts to introduce sustainability into projects at my company are perceived," or "I lead a City green building team, and feel I could be more effective." Or it can be at the broader, organizational level, such as "We're

Figure 12.6

planning our succession, and want to make sure the next generation of owners carry on, and perhaps enhance, our sustainability initiatives." Or it can be even more far-reaching, such as "I'm working on a state-wide initiative, and don't feel I have a strong enough coalition to succeed." To issues such as these, we identify a desired deliverable – for example, a plan for building that coalition in the latter case – and conditions that must be taken into consideration when developing that deliverable. These conditions often act as constraints, but not always. Sometimes they can be re-invented as an asset.

For individuals who are "living" the particular scenario back at their workplace or in their community – the scenario team planning process can be very helpful – they often leave with their group's planning flip charts in hand with every intention to use them (with the group's permission, of course). And their team members get to enjoy when the scenario becomes realized successfully.

Below is a recent example of one scenario we have used. (More examples will be provided as part of "bonus" materials on the EMERGE Leadership Website.) Notice that it includes a description of the situation, a deliverable that needs to be created, and conditions that must be considered (groups can add to, but not delete conditions).

When Miracles Are Needed

I briefly mentioned Transformative Scenario Planning (TSP) above, a method practiced and promoted by Adam Kahane. It's a tool I've adapted for work with organizations that are "stuck." Kahane has developed TSP to address complex and difficult situations among parties that don't necessarily trust each other, one example being reconciliation in post-apartheid South

Scenario: Changing a Company's Priorities

You work for a well-run development company with good people, interesting tasks, and a positive working environment. The organization has a fair-sized building portfolio; but sustainability is not a priority. You'd like to invest some time and energy into turning this around. There is an annual firm-wide meeting where employees are invited to make visionary proposals. Please address the following conditions:

- Your company leadership needs to be convinced to spend some money upfront to "green" its operations, staff, and development investments.
- A few of your colleagues have obtained LEED or similar green building accreditations, but their practices have not changed. Other colleagues have seen no need to learn about sustainable building.
- The organization's public relations department sees the value of "green" in the political environment, but does not have a comprehensive understanding of the subject.
- You are not part of the management team; however one of the partners has shown an interest in mentoring you.
- You have an adorable new baby at home, and a partner that would like to see you on occasion.

Africa. In his book *Transformative Scenario Planning* Kahane relates a joke that was prevalent during that era: "Faced with our country's overwhelming problems," the joke went, "we have only two options: a practical option and a miraculous option. The practical option (for post-apartheid planners) would be for 'all of us to get down on our knees and pray for a band of angels to come down from heaven and solve our problem for us. The miraculous option would be for us to talk and work together and find a way forward together'" (Kahane 2012, 4). When I read this passage, my first thought was that global climate change seems to require a miracle that is slow in coming and that TSP should be employed there. (Better start praying!)

TSP uses the tool of story to help break through stuck thinking about the way things are and the way things could be. In conventional scenario planning, planners identify what scenarios are likely to happen, and work out how to make the best of these scenarios. In transformative scenario planning, participants are asked to explore what could be, using the framework of storytelling. *It adds aspiration into the mix!* And instead of just anticipating and adapting, it looks for ways to influence or transform. I was not surprised to read that Kahane considers the Transformative Scenario process "as a whole...an *emergent* process" and that it includes divergent and convergent steps, such as those we in the sustainable building world consider important to successfully achieving Integrative Design (IP, see Chapter 10) (Kahane 2012, 46).

TSP starts at the mindset level and works through process to shift mindset. The process transforms the actors' understanding, relationships, intentions, and actions (Kahane 2012, 18). It includes five steps: 1) creating a whole system team; 2) observing what is happening; 3) constructing stories of positive possibility; 4) discovering what can and must be done; and 5) taking action. (Kahane 2012, 22).

Even when we are not addressing huge problems such as peace in the Sudan, or global climate change, we can use this tool. I used it, in a much simplified and abbreviated form, when working with a 20-year old regional non-profit. Some of the group's chapters had begun to work independently, and not always in concert with each other or the regional charter. Some of the group's chapters had simply faded away and were no longer functioning.

The Board Chair created a team to work through the problem, which threatened the overall viability of this very important organization. We met in retreat for a day, the day before the organization's formal Board meeting. I facilitated a discussion that focused on what was happening to and within their organization, helping them avoid the tendency to focus on how they could fix it (the topic of improving the website – note the devolution into tool/technology talk -- proved alluring at times). Once we had a shared understanding of the current story, we broke up in to smaller teams to come up with alternatives, complete with titles and story lines. In this case three story lines were developed, one in which the regional Board continued to lead the organization with chapters acting independently (but cooperating more), one in which the chapters became independent organizations entirely, and one in which the regional entity and chapters worked much more collaboratively. As a whole the group wanted to explore the last story line, or scenario, more.

Through the ensuing discussion, they realized how much their mental model for the organization was playing into what they were experiencing. For years the regional entity has thought of themselves as an umbrella organization, with chapters under the umbrella. Other than the shelter of the umbrella, there was nothing keeping the entire entity – regional and local – together. They needed a new mental model, which would support the new story. With me they explored imagery that was more inclusive and more representative of their desire to collaborate regionally. They continued this discussion without me at the Regional Board meeting the next day. There, they came up with the image of a house, with each of the chapters representing rooms in the house. And because they philosophically see buildings as systems, this was a perfect mental model for them to work with. They were dealing with a system, and now the primary system elements had clear relationships with each other.

Not surprisingly, I heard later from several Board members that "it was the best Board meeting in years!" It was as if an ice dam had broken. Obviously it was just the beginning. Even if we'd spent the months required for a formal TSP process, the kind of systemic change they were contemplating could take a long time.

Collective Impact: Where Learning Together Can Address Complex Issues

As part of their preparation for the EMERGE Leadership workshop, I ask attendees to read "Embracing Emergence: How Collective Impact

Addresses Complexity," by John Kania and Mark Kramer in the *Stanford Social Innovation Review* (Kania and Kramer 2013).

Collective Impact is a term Kania and Kramer have made popular, and which has come to signify a particular and highly structured approach to addressing cross-sector social problems. It's another tool where learning together can help solve problems, and especially complex ones.

In their social change work, consultants Kania and Kramer recognized that "no single organization is responsible for a major social problem, nor can any single organization cure it." So they developed a model for cross-sector problem solving that includes five conditions: a common agenda, shared measurement, mutually reinforcing activities, continuous communication, and a coordinating entity they call the "backbone." They liken these conditions to the "rules" that operate when birds are flocking: "maintain a minimum distance from your neighbor; fly at the same speed as your neighbor; and always turn towards the center."

When human communities intentionally apply the conditions of *Collective Impact*, they "see as one" and can more easily act as one – becoming more effective. To date, the Collective Impact approach has been applied primarily to social issues such as education, health, and safety. It's easy to see, however, how this might apply to some of the knottier environmental problems we are trying to solve with our movement. A "common agenda" in our realm might be addressing climate change through energy efficiency and use of renewables. The organizations that might be part

of a Collective Impact coalition in this case would include the usual suspects, i.e., a climate-change oriented NGO, a community energy efficiency program, local government. But the coalition could also include the local building contractors group, design professionals, affordable housing authorities, workforce development and training institutions, and any other group that by their decisions and actions impact the ability of the community to improve the energy efficiency of buildings and optimize the use of renewables. By enlarging the "flock," so to speak, and by improving the ability to fly in unison – through the backbone organization – more resources are available and opportunities for new and better solutions arise.

According to Kania and Kramer, "having a shared understanding of the problem and an appropriately framed common agenda increases the likelihood that communities will see relevant opportunities as they emerge. The novelty of working with people from different sectors brings a fresh perspective that encourages creativity and intensifies effort. And sharing fresh perspectives, in turn, can motivate more generous support from both participants and outsiders. The rules for interaction from Collective Impact create an alignment within complex relationships and sets

of activities which, when combined with shared intentionality, causes previously invisible solutions and resources to emerge" (Kania and Mark 2013, 2-3).

In this chapter, we have discussed the importance of shared, joyful learning to effective, emergent collaboration. Kania and Kramer offer a context for emergent collaboration on a large scale, and it's applicable to addressing some of the most complex issues of our time. Notably, one of the benefits they discuss is the "simultaneous learning" that happens in Collective Impact initiatives (Kania and Mark, 2013, 5). In traditional social change structures, individual organizations learn and act independently (to the degree that they can). Picture multiple flocks flying with different flight plans! I believe that a Collective Impact approach has great potential for our movement. In May 2013, I facilitated a leadership roundtable convened by the Hawaii Chapter of the U. S. Green Building Council at that state's annual Buy and Build Green Conference. The purpose of the event was to discuss opportunities to cooperate and build collective impact. As in the climate change example above, the invitation list went beyond the typical "green building" activists. It was limited to non-governmental nonprofits, but any organization whose mission touched on "improving the quality of life through influencing the built environment" in some manner was invited to send a representative. Every aspect of the residential and commercial building and design industry was represented at the conference by the nearly 20 attendees from AIA, ASID, ASLA, GCA, BIA, CSI, IADA, APA, NIAP, ULI, and BOMA.

Hawaii is not a huge community, but when I asked when the last time was that these organizations had met to discuss the topic at hand, attendees looked at each other and laughed a little sheepishly. Many of the participating organizations were decades-old, and all had worked in various ways to improve the quality of the built environment. Several of those attending were long-time friends. But on the issue of creating a sustainable built environment that "works for all,"

they had never met. While acknowledging each of the individual organizations' historic contributions to this cause, all agreed that working together – and in particular sharing information – would bring significant collective benefits to the organizations, and to Hawaii as a whole. Though brief (the event was 1.5 hours) the discussion resulted in a unanimous decision to bring the idea of developing a common agenda back to their respective organizations.

Although this local organizational cooperation would clearly not fulfill all of Kania and Kramer's conditions for Collective Impact, we can see how the concept might be useful in improving the impact of a given community's sustainable building initiatives, simply by getting more players in the room, learning as peers.

What Meeting Planners Need to Know

First, every meeting should have a purpose. No-one should be wondering why they are in the room.

Second, just like a building, every meeting should have a plan. The agenda is the plan for the meeting. An annotated agenda (Figure 12.7) is developed by the meeting planners with input from any of those expected to contribute to portions of the meeting. It can be multiple pages, and will include details on any activities planned, supplies needed for those activities, and who is responsible for both leading and making sure preparations are completed. The handout agenda (Figure 12.8) should be simple – one page is best – with schedule, topics, and persons responsible for presenting or leading that section of the agenda. I've generally created this only after we've perfected the annotated agenda. (Please note that Figures 12.7 and 12.8 are for visual reference only. Full-sized examples of both the annotated agenda and the handout are available with bonus book materials; see Author's Final Note for access information.)

Third, in building that agenda, there should be opportunities to connect, opportunities to learn, and opportunities to optimize the DNA in the room. Create easy ways for everyone to participate. Give shy persons a running start. The more engaged meeting participants are, the more productive they will be, and the more likely they will follow through on meeting outcomes.

Fourth, planning should include a healthy discussion of who needs to be at the meeting to effectively meet the meeting's purpose. Sometimes involving key players in presenting or facilitating meeting segments can ensure your meeting is getting the attention it deserves.

Fifth, thought should be given to the venue, the food, the materials. Walk the talk: make sustainable choices when it comes to where you meet, the food you serve, the supplies you use, the means you or others have to use to get to the venue.

And finally, every meeting should be a model of respect and servant leadership. Plan enough time for the meeting, paring the agenda down to make sure no one is rushed, everyone who wants to gets to contribute, and your meeting ends on time. Be there early enough to set it up properly, provide reasonable breaks, and acknowledge everyone with a thank-you, when you start, and when you conclude. None of this is rocket science, and yet–.

City Sustainability Strategy
City Staff Workshop Agenda
May 12, 2010

Time	Agenda Item	Who	Logistics/ Notes
8:30 AM	Project Overview & Purpose of Workshop	Jane	Review agenda, seat in breakout groups.
8:40	City Sustainability Planning Presentation • Sustainability 101 • Sustainability Strategy Overview & Examples • Sustainable City • City Department Sustainability Inventory	Kathleen & Jane	Kathleen presents PPT. References: Physical samples of what other cities are doing, Printed inventory developed by Jane of current departmental/city efforts. Laptop, LCD Projector, screen/surface
9:05	A Sustainable City – What Should We Prioritize? Interactive Exercise Part I • Sustainable Priorities (Categories)	Kathleen	Kathleen presents printed worksheet. Breakout groups identify facilitator, scribe, and reporter. Groups are assigned discussion of Question 1 on the worksheet. Scribe to capture all comments of the group directly on the worksheet. References: Definitions Handout. "Bike Rack" Easel/Flip Chart: to capture individual contributions outside of their assignment.
9:15	A Sustainable City – What Should We Prioritize Interactive Exercise Part II • Sustainable Priorities (Goals)	Kathleen	Groups are assigned discussion of Question 2 on the worksheet. Scribe to capture all comments of the group directly on the worksheet. Remind them of difference between control and influence. Focus on control. Inform participants that a follow-up electronic survey will be sent to individuals to get more detailed responses to the above questions (digging a bit deeper), and to get interdepartmental and interdisciplinary feedback on suggested priorities and actions compiled across the multiple workshops. Test water for concept of "green team". References: Mind Map showing relationship of categories and goals. "Bike Rack" Easel/Flip Chart: to capture individual contributions outside of their assignment.

811 First Avenue, Suite 360 · Seattle, WA 98104 · 206-621-8626 · www.obrienandco.com

Figure 12.7

City Sustainability Strategy
City Staff Workshop Agenda
May 12, 2010
8:30am – 10:00am

Time	Agenda Item	Who
8:30 AM	Project Overview & Purpose of Workshop	Jane
8:40	City Sustainability Planning Presentation	Kathleen & Jane
9:05	A Sustainable City – What Should We Prioritize?	Kathleen
9:15	A Sustainable City – What Should We Prioritize	Kathleen
9:55	Let's Get Fired Up!	Jane
10:00	Wrap up and Adjourn	Jane

Figure 12.8

Building a Beloved Community

Recapping the Community component of the EMERGE Leadership Model, the foundation is *collaboration*, the centerpiece is *learning*, and the distinction is *caring* – or, to be more courageous, *love*. (Figure 13.1) An emergent leader understands that leadership is a "we" activity. This is obvious when we practice emergent collaboration, where any sustained positive impact is the work of a collective imagination and will, aided by sweat, circumstances, and grace. Love (often expressed as mutual respect and the camaraderie that exists as a result of shared experiences) has a clear place in fostering such collaboration, whether we are thinking about project teams, business structures, or community initiatives. The emergent collaborative approach makes explicit the intent to create joyful, mindful experiences in which participants learn, grow in leadership capacity, and imagine restorative solutions that represent true progress towards a sustainable society.

Figure 13.1

In this chapter, however, I want to discuss another aspect of this "we-ness." In my leadership efforts I have never achieved any good result by myself; and I would be lying if I said I did. I rely on my friends, colleagues, and mentors for advice and support in good times, and bad. Therefore, the focus here is on how we as leaders need community to sustain ourselves, to thrive in our leadership.

Emergent Leaders Need Community

The paradox is that to be an effective leader, one must rely on others. In *Leadership and the New Science*, Wheatley writes that "each organism maintains a clear sense of its individual identity *within* a larger network of relationships that help shape its identity" and that "we survive only as we learn how to participate in a web of relationships" (Wheatley 2006, 20). She expands further on this life-making phenomenon, known as *autopoiesis*, as "one in which all organisms are capable of creating a 'self' through their intimate engagement with all others in their system" (Wheatley 2006, 20). To very loosely paraphrase: Emergent Leaders create themselves through intimate engagement with others with whom they interact.

In *Teachings on Love*, Thich Nhat Hanh notes, "If you are a psychotherapist, a doctor, a social worker, a peace worker, or if you are working for the environment, you need a *Sangha*. Without a Sangha, you will not have enough support, and you will burn out very soon" (Nhat Hanh 1998, 138). Sangha is most commonly used to describe a Buddhist monastic community. Obviously Thich Nhat Hanh is not suggesting we all become Buddhists; I believe he is using the word Sangha for its root meaning: "assembly" or "community" ("Sangha" July 10, 2015).

Joanna Macy and Chris Johnstone in *Active Hope* ask, "How can we remain fired up for any length of time without being driven to exhaustion?" (Macy and Johnstone 2012, 213). We can't. Burnout is something anyone proposing a change away from "business as usual" is likely to encounter. I certainly have – and more than once. One of the reasons I grew O'Brien & Company beyond a home- office consulting business was because of the loneliness and even despair I sometimes felt in my work. Sure, my forward-thinking clients offered some nourishment in this regard. I recall long phone calls with clients, generally public or nonprofit employees, who were facing similar frustrations and challenges within their institutions or in their outreach efforts. (We were, after all, breaking entirely new ground!) But by expanding my business, I was able to build a team with whom I could share ideas, build enthusiasm, and address concerns together. If I needed to re-boot when burnout threatened, I was in the position to do so. I could "vent" safely – and sometimes my O'Brien & Company colleagues would be the first to suggest I needed a break!

Being Glum Isn't "Attractive"

It is important to seek out "encouragement, aid, and good counsel," say Macy and Johnstone. By doing so, "we create a more favorable context both for our projects and for ourselves" (Macy and Johnstone 2012, 201).

Developing a support network around us (or finding one and contributing to it) is important to keep us going. But it's not just about us. If we present a positive, robust, even happy prospect to those whom we hope to influence (i.e., those we are hoping to lead), we are much more likely to enroll them in our efforts. "There is a strategic value to making what we do rewarding, and it goes further than preventing just burnout.... The [environmental] movement needs to grow, and the attractiveness of participation grows when it is recognized as a path to deepened aliveness and a more satisfying way of life" (Macy and Johnstone 2012, 213).

I had to learn the hard way that attraction, rather than "promotion," was the better, and more effective, form of leadership. No one wants to be told what to do, especially by a sourpuss!

In Chapter 11, we discussed the importance of joyful learning (or play) to finding more creative solutions. When we are happy, we do better work. Macy and Johnstone say something similar: "[t]he more we get absorbed in an activity, the better we get at it" (Macy and Johnstone 2012, 219). Therefore, we need to maintain happiness in our work as much as we can. Thich Nhat Hanh has said, "[h]appiness is not an individual matter" (Hanh, 1998, 55).

In his treatise on play, Stuart Brown says we are happy "when we can live an expansive life, one in which we are aware that we are actively participating in something greater than ourselves." But the examples of "greater-than-ourselves" experiences Brown then gives are not what you might expect, i.e., saving the planet, saving someone's life, creating a very successful green building program.

Rather, these experiences are all about relationship – as with a "couple, friendship, or family, or within an intellectual, social, or spiritual community" (Brown and Vaughn 2009, 201).

This isn't about sitting in a circle happily singing "Kumbaya" – although there is nothing wrong with that! "We are simply more effective when acting from strengths and enthusiasm" (Macy and Johnstone 2012, 218). And working with the support of community provides both.

Earlier, in Chapter 3, I described true sustainability as thriving, not just surviving. As professionals dedicated to creating and/or restoring life-sustaining environments, we too need to focus on our own thriving, not simply surviving. Our work will be more personally satisfying and professionally rewarding if we connect to and participate in a positive, caring, supportive community.

TRANSFORMATION IN PRACTICE:
Enterprise Community

Enterprise's story is one of an organization that has envisioned transformation in society while allowing itself to evolve. Whether or not it was a conscious choice in its beginnings in 1973, the organization and the visionaries leading it and working within it have clearly listened "to what the system (was telling it)," as suggested by Donella Meadows in her book *Thinking in Systems*. They were discovering how its properties and the organization's values can work together to bring forth something much better than could ever be produced by the organization's will alone (paraphrasing Meadows 2006, 169-170).

In 1973, Jim Rouse and colleagues created a social enterprise that would seek to "move people out of poverty" as well as "continue working until everyone in [the U.S.] had a safe and affordable place to call home." Today Enterprise is a family of companies working together to build opportunity in communities across the U.S. These companies lend funds, finance development, manage properties and build affordable housing. They partner with national and local groups to create programs that strengthen community. They advance policies to increase

the supply and quality of affordable housing and make it possible for individuals and businesses to support housing and community development by donating charitable dollars and investing in socially responsible funds and tax credits. All of this transformative work has translated into real, lasting impact (Enterprise 2015).

Simply creating good quality affordable housing is itself deeply transformative, and an excellent example of how buildings can impact individual lives and the communities in which those individuals live. From its inception Enterprise has been improving both the quality and quantity of affordable housing. By the early 2000s they had influenced the renovation or construction of many thousands of housing units across the U.S.. At the same time, Enterprise was hearing from its stakeholders that the definition of quality might need to be expanded to include environmentally sensitive criteria. In 2004, it launched Enterprise Green Communities, a program that would provide such criteria as well as technical assistance and funding to help non-profit housing developers meet them. Enterprise's "green" initiative would continue to grow, as the resolve in 2004 was to ensure all the properties in which Enterprise invested would be developed with the Enterprise Green Communities criteria, and that by 2020 all the properties Enterprise owned would meet them. According to Krista Eggers, Senior Program Director of Enterprise Green Communities, the organization is "on track" to meet this audacious goal (Eggers August 13, 2015). The new Oxford Plaza Project developed by Resources for Community Development (RCD), a non-profit affordable housing developer in the San Francisco Bay area, California is just one of many new projects contributing to this goal. (See photo, opposite page.)

Meanwhile the organization has not shied from improving the criteria to reflect what it was learning from the field. Eggers notes that "the organization's definition of what constitutes 'green' has evolved considerably: While in 2004 the focus was primarily on energy performance, water efficiency, and waste reduction, the criteria now includes a much stronger emphasis on health and community resilience." A good part of this effort is due to having "much better data about the potential impact of the built environment on resident and staff's health exists; at the same time, more information about the threat of climate change and related environmental crises and how buildings can contribute to them – and can protect communities from them through resilient features – has become available" (Eggers August 13, 2015). The latest rendition of the criteria has actually taken a step beyond "what even market-rate green building programs have been able to do," says Alistair Jackson of O'Brien & Company, "by, in addition to including health-supporting features and resilient design options, enhancing integrative process requirements to improve the likelihood of project teams achieving intended outcomes" (Jackson August 25, 2015).

In developing these criteria, the organization invested in good quality input. Says Jackson, "Enterprise acknowledged that it can be hard for subject matter experts to carve out time to contribute to these program update processes; in the most recent update (in 2015) they provided stipends for participation, freeing contributors to commit quality time to the development process" (Jackson August 25, 2015). In a field where it is common for certification programs to rely on volunteer contributions, this approach is refreshing.

Another change that has occurred within the Green Communities initiative is the recognition – again because of what stakeholders began telling them – that their focus needed to move beyond bricks and mortar. "What our developers, designers, and asset managers were telling us was that that they'd figured out how to design and build green buildings to the criteria; the problem was the back end – the operation of green buildings. We realized we needed to start looking at people, not buildings, if we were to provide the quality of life benefits we were hoping to" (Eggers 2015).

This change of focus meant engaging residents in the new initiative as well as operating staff. O'Brien & Company was involved in both as it helped develop and pilot customizable residential engagement materials and a green O&M manual and training in 2011.

In 2011, we interviewed Maria Elena Marquez-Brookes, LINC Housing's Director of Resident Services, to see how the residential engagement initiative was going. LINC is a nonprofit developer of affordable housing for low-income seniors, families and individuals with special needs throughout the state of California, and one of five non-profit affordable housing agencies that participated in Enterprise's residential engagement pilot program. LINC and the other pilot participants helped review, test, and refine a set of customizable "Resident Engagement Cards" that could be used as posters, printed guides, presentations, and more (examples from the LINC pilot are shown). Marques-Brookes reported being surprised at the level of engagement in their first meeting, which used 5 of the 30 cards they had customized and focused on introducing simple energy saving actions they could take, as well as introducing ideas like creating a "green" all purpose household cleaning product. "We were a little surprised; since we held it directly following our after school program, we expected youth to stay and participate. We didn't really expect adults to come. It was a two-hour meeting on a weeknight, dinner included. We had 27 participants, including 15 kids and 12 adults ranging in age from 7 years old to someone in their 60's. We had moms, dads, grandparents, and whole families participating, and everyone stayed right to the end." (Marquez-Brookes April 6, 2011).

RCD, the San Francisco-based affordable housing developer mentioned above, also participated in the pilot. The organization works hard to provide high quality "green" housing for low income households priced out of the housing market in the Bay Area. RCD used the residential engagement tools to create posters prominently displayed in their facilities. In addition their initial orientation and newsletters provide information on how residents and staff can save energy, reduce waste, and stay healthy. RCD and other affordable housing providers have benefited from translations of the residential engagement materials provided by Enterprise through its website. The "cards" referenced above by Marquez-Brookes are now available in Armenian, Korean, Arabic, and Spanish, among other languages.

One of the outcomes of the pilot involvement with RCD was the realization that the organization's outsourced property management was a potential pitfall. In order to ensure that contracted property managers supported the ideas being promoted through residential engagement education – and didn't unwittingly sabotage them – Enterprise hired my firm to conduct a workshop for the property managers. The John Stewart Company, RCD's property management agent, realized this was good business and proposed that the training be extended to PMs working for other affordable housing non-profits. Thanks to Enterprise support, instead of the initial eight PMs, nearly 60 PMs attended, making a significantly larger positive impact.

The increased emphasis on "people" can be seen in the recent update of the Enterprise Green Community Criteria: residential engagement and operator guidance are directly woven into the criteria, with encouragement to start engagement and educational activities much earlier in the process. In addition, the criteria reveal a greater focus on active living (for better resident and staff health) as well as resilience.

Krista Eggers: "Our work now with residential engagement tools is to make sure they can be completely integrated into the fabric of a particular situation. In addition, our stakeholders are telling us that it's the kids that will make this happen. We have housing agencies 'doubling-down' on their commitments, with an eye on making a difference to younger and future generations."

Enterprise continues to allow itself to change, as opportunities to transform our society through greening affordable housing emerge. It's a great example of transformation in practice.

Photo (Credit): Treve Johnson Photography
Links:
http://www.enterprisecommunity.com/solutions-and-innovation/enterprise-green-communities/criteria-and-certification
http://www.enterprisecommunity.com/solutions-and-innovations/enterprise-green-communities/tools-and-services

Getting Started

At this point, you might be wondering if you have what it takes to be an emergent leader. I guarantee you, you do.

The point of developing an "emergent" leadership model rather than a linear one is to provide the basis for *anyone* with the willingness, discipline, and native intelligence to lead effectively. The level of environmental degradation, societal distress, and economic disparity experienced in our world today presents an urgent, toxic combination, which can only be addressed systematically, from multiple points in the various systems involved. We need more effective leaders and we need lots of them.

The EMERGE Leadership Model provides a context in which more individuals dedicated to true sustainability - no matter what their position in the particular "systems" in which they participate - can develop a leadership style that both suits them and grows others to do the same. It is a leadership model intended to help build the capacity to lead more effectively at the personal, organizational, and community level in order to create lasting positive change. In this chapter, we discuss how you might get started applying the concepts to your situation on the personal level, and briefly discuss how you might take this leadership to your community. In Chapter 15, we'll discuss how the concepts apply at the organizational level.

Personal Leadership Development Plan

Emergent leadership allows you to lead in a way that reflects your unique strengths, not someone else's. Of course, that means you need to understand what your strengths are, and identify ways to expand on them and utilize them. It also means you need to become aware of your limitations, not so much to force yourself to eliminate them, but to avoid trying to be something/someone you are not. (I will never be a tall, white man with a booming voice, for example, but I'm really creative, persistent as heck, and have a kooky sense of humor that allows me to make a fool of myself when that's what it takes!)

Becoming an emergent leader is closely aligned with the maturing process. It is very grown up, for example, to focus on service and growth of others, to focus on results and not on kudos, to witness rather than judge, to develop foresight muscles rather than relying simply on impulse. I can tell you that developing any of these skills was a real stretch for me, and sometimes I was just lucky! I am also grateful for colleagues who were willing to be honest with me.

This maturation process is less a matter of age than experience, although it does take some time to garner experiences! In my life, I have found that willingness to consult with more experienced individuals can help fill the gap age might represent. (Recall the discussion of mentoring, Chapter 4.) And motivation can be an impressive tool! I have seen remarkable examples of younger EMERGE workshop participants achieving great things.

Near the conclusion of our intensive EMERGE Leadership workshops, we offer a quiet period for participants to draft their "personal leadership development plan." This work includes self-evaluation, an opportunity to identify a particular area of leadership focus, as well as a plan to enhance the skills necessary to excel in that focus, and finally a 90-day plan to kick-start the process of executing their plan. (The form for completing your personal leadership development plan is provided in Appendix A. An editable PDF version is available to anyone who has purchased the book along with other "bonus materials." See Author's Final Note for access.)

Readers will notice that the 90-day plan includes identifying allies, reflecting the critical need for support we discussed in Chapter 12. Readers will also notice the direction to include steps to grow emotionally, cognitively, and spiritually. In the context of our leadership development, this can be defined as feeling, thinking, and acting in ways that are in alignment with emergent leadership principles. For example, how do your feelings, thoughts, and actions line up with the intention to serve and grow those you lead?

Probably the most important outcome of your personal leadership development planning process is to clearly understand your "why." Why do you want to lead? What are you leading towards? In a mentoring session, a bright young architect shared her desire to be a motivational speaker and writer. Nothing wrong with that. But when I asked her, "For what purpose, specifically?" she had nothing more than the broad vision of sustainability and regenerative thinking motivating *her*. I encouraged her to think about the specific outcomes she would like from her (future) motivational work. Being more specific about your "why" is incredibly helpful when designing your personal leadership plan. For example, you may discover some areas of research you need to conduct to provide greater credibility for your leadership work. Or you may understand better the specific relationships you need to cultivate, and be more strategic with informational interviews you might plan.

What is Your Why?

So what is your why? Although I have confessed to being an "accidental" leader, I actually like planning, and have taken advantage of all sorts of tools to help me sort out how to approach dealing with challenges I was facing. Elizabeth Powers, my colleague at O'Brien & Company, would tell new employee, "If you want to connect with Kathleen, take her a problem, she loves working on problems!" The personal leadership

development plan reflects what I've learned works for me. But finding out *your* why requires a bit more than simply filling it out on a form.

There are self-help books and blogs out there to help you with this process. I'm going to suggest a very simple routine. At the end of each day, notice what about the day enlivened you, and what about the day drained you. Write it down. You'll notice patterns. Then you can explore these patterns using any number of tools. I like mind-mapping. Although it's ordinarily used for business or project planning, as shown in Figure 14.1, it actually is a wonderful tool for exploring you and your purpose. A mind-map can help you connect those apparently disconnected things you have found are enlivening or joyful. For example, if you find joy in researching things, and in addition to

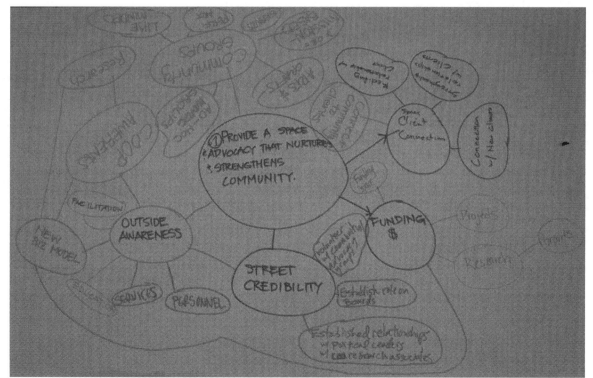

Figure 14.1

that you enjoy figuring out how to repurpose things, and in addition to that you like to work with others on social justice, you might want to figure out how to work with the affordable housing community to fund research that would foster rehabilitation of existing buildings for low-income populations. Just a thought!

Planning is a proactive activity. But to make a good plan, it's important to utilize what you intuitively understand, and that means taking the time to observe what is happening in quiet. Earlier in the book, I have discussed *witnessing*, the non-judgmental observation of "what's happening." In a recent mentoring session, we practically galloped through a mind-mapping session of an experienced city planner's interests. I ended the session, however, with the suggestion that planning is great, but "things happen" – and to take advantage of this fortuitous aspect of life. In a subsequent session, she noted that indeed a couple of "things" had happened that had informed her planning.

I am often asked how I got where I've gotten in my career. My response has been that "I saw a buoy and I swam to it…, I saw another buoy, and swam to that one…, and so forth." But of course, there's a reason that particular buoy called to me. And a reason I was willing to swim to it, even if the water seemed cold and filled with dreaded unknowns. (cue the "Jaws" theme.)

One of the things that helped me improve my ability to both "see" the buoy and "swim" to it was to discover and commit to developing something Doug Lennick and Fred Kiel call "moral intelligence." They define moral intelligence as "the ability to differentiate

right from wrong as defined by universal principles… [which are] those beliefs about human conduct that are common to all cultures around the world… [and which] apply to all people, regardless of gender, ethnicity, religious belief, or location on the globe" (Lennick and Kiel 2005, xxxiii). Although my journey long preceded the publication of this book, I was lucky in my early 30s to find spiritual resources that helped me locate and calibrate my moral compass. I had to learn what those universal principles are, and when I was swimming towards them, and when I was swimming away from them.

Finding My Way

The universal principles Lennick and Kiel refer to (such as empathy, responsibility, and reciprocity) act as my "true north" (Lennick and Kiel 2005, 20). It is far easier to moderate my behavior when I understand what gets me there, and what doesn't. For example, I've learned that if I feel compulsively driven to doing something (right now!) that my best course of action is to PAUSE. It's in the pause that I discover what I should truly be doing with whatever the situation presented to me is. In looking back, I realize that this behavior is an important aspect of foresight, which we've already discussed as an important characteristic of effective leadership.

Say Lennick and Kiel, "while moral intelligence involves *knowing* what to do, moral competence is the skill of actually *doing* the right thing…. We need it to understand what goals will allow us to be true to our principles, and we need [it] to act in alignment with our value and beliefs" (Lennick & Kiel 2005, 65). The business authors provide a worksheet for conducting a Moral Competency Inventory in their book *Moral*

Intelligence. (Lennick and Kiel 2005, 227).

The authors also stress that in order to be morally competent, one must be emotionally competent. "Emotional competence...helps us understand our own emotions, especially those that can get in the way of doing the right thing" (Lennick and Kiel 2005, 66). The regular awareness practices suggested in Chapter 7 of this book can help you both discover where you are, and where you'd like to be in terms of your behavior – which is a direct outcome of how you deal with your emotions, as well as how clearly you understand the principles or values that drive you.

The key is to remain teachable. "[We need to] shift away from the idea that there is one right way forward that we all follow…, [and] each of us needs to find our place of greatest fit" (Macy and Johnstone 2012, 218). Finding our place of greatest fit is an iterative process, just as good quality design is.

Getting Help

Regardless, just as the leadership work itself requires us to be in community, the act of planning our leadership path is one we should undertake with the help of others. In an interview conducted by On Being's Krista Tippett with Dr. Imani Perry on the subject of race, community, and the American consciousness, Perry says, "the work of nurturing development always requires us to lean on someone else, or to be there for someone else to lean on, to facilitate, to nurture it." Perry's perspective applies to our own planning process as well. In the interview she says, "We are being socialized into intense competition…, every aspect of our lives is marketized. [This market competition] creates a lot of anxiety…

because we don't want to be left behind and left out." But the other side of this "anxiety is that it really isolates us from a sense of responsibility." Imani urges us to think about the image of a splint supporting a living sprout. Sometimes we are the splint, sometimes the sprout. She also stresses in the interview that the splint is not "compensating, simply helping the living sprout come into its own" (Perry 2011).

How does this work in real time? Letting go of the idea we are competing for attention, a big job, a new title, and asking for help in identifying our why, and developing our plan. Further, by being ready to reciprocate when asked. Not to say you should do this "willy-nilly." This is an important relationship and trust is and should be involved. Again, listening to yourself and to the colleague or friend you are approaching is critical to determining if this is a contract you want to make.

As emergent leaders we need to be resilient. "To strengthen our resilience, we need to pay attention to all of the factors that sustain us" (Macy and Johnstone 2012, 215). Again, we are asked to be observant. An honest, and non-judging witness of what is happening is the stance of an emergent leader.

Taking Your Leadership to Your Community

Many readers are professionals hoping to utilize emergent leadership concepts in their work-life. However, it's often the case that the same individuals are active in sustainable initiatives in their local communities as volunteers. The EMERGE Leadership Model applies equally well in those circumstances, as do the techniques. And just as emergent leadership skills and dispositions help you succeed in your professional life whether you have title or position, they will help you whether you are a volunteer leader/facilitator or simply a stakeholder.

For example, Chapter 11 presents emergent collaboration, and advises you if you are in the position of outside consultant facilitating a collaborative process. What if you are simply one of a number of volunteers participating in that process? For one thing, you can make suggestions to the facilitator/consultant along the lines of the guidance presented in this book, and in particular, along the lines of emergent collaboration. You can also model emergent leadership in any activities you participate in, for example, if voluntarily facilitating small group breakouts or coordinating an activity leading towards the overarching goal.

This is the case in your professional community or communities as well. Like it or not, even green building non-profits that rely heavily on volunteers don't necessarily exhibit anything close to emergent leadership behaviors. As one of those volunteers, you can do this organization – and our planet! – a favor by taking these concepts with you to your meetings and events.

Why You Want to Be an Agent Of Change and Not Necessarily a Change Agent

When I was thinking about what to call the form of leadership this book is about, I struggled with many of the terms we bandy about in the field of social change, including what we call someone doing this work. One of them, which I've frequently used myself, is the term "change agent." I've had the pleasure of working with Janine Benyus as my Independent Study "evaluator" while pursuing my Masters in 2000-2002. (Like some others, I was exploring how Biomimicry concepts might be applied to the green building realm.) Among other things, Janine was relentless in terms of making sure I wasn't sloppy with scientific terminology, especially terms that derive from nature. Anyone who's met Janine probably knows that she wants us to be very thoughtful when we apply the term "Bio-mimicry."

Janine is the reason I've used the term "emergence," because as a natural phenomenon it more precisely represents what I want to convey.

Janine's tutelage and my innate tendency as a writer/editor to gravitate towards precise language led me to reflect carefully as I thought about naming the leadership concept I was promoting, as well as the individual applying it. Emergence, which I define early in the book as the natural phenomenon where simple and identical elements come together to form unique, elegant, and often functional systems, seemed to fit perfectly.

So what about the term "change agent"? I'm not convinced it's appropriate for the kind of leadership I'm promoting. If you search the internet, you will find that a change agent is someone (inside or outside) an organization that helps it transform itself, usually by focusing on organizational effectiveness. There's a tremendous amount of support in leadership literature for using the term change agent and for figuring out how you can be one. But I believe the term originated from the idea of chemical (change) agents or reagents. Such agents do cause change. However, they can often disappear altogether in the change because they are consumed, or they don't change at all, so the analogy breaks down. With emergent Leadership, I'm hoping that you will not only stick around, but will learn as you go. I *want* you to change, and for the better. At the same time the concept of emergent leadership honors your unique "you-ness." It encourages you to develop leadership skills and dispositions in alignment with your core. So I've begun resisting the easy use of the term change agent, and am hoping that as emergent Leaders you are instead *agents of change*.

All this is not to argue for dropping "change agent" from leadership vocabulary. Plenty of good people like and use the term. It's more about being thoughtful and attentive with the language you use, both to describe yourself and your "version" of emergent leadership, as well as to communicate with the prospective servant-leaders or emergent leaders you are cultivating.

Emergence at the Organizational Level

There are dozens, if not hundreds of books offering advice on organizational leadership and how to develop it. (Again, my favorites on these and other topics are listed with other bonus materials. See Author's Final Note for access information.) In this final chapter, just as we have in the rest of this book, our focus is on leadership with the ultimate goal of a life-sustaining built environment. How might emergent leadership be applied or represented in organizations?

Most obviously, the organization should include in its mission or goal statements a desire to contribute to a more sustainable built environment. This intention can be expressed through action in the following, and ideally all, ways: in the work the organization does; in the way the organization conducts that work; and in the way the organization operates internally.

One may assume that in order to foster emergent leadership within an organization, one needs be in a position of authority. Organizational Psychologist Meisha Rouser believes otherwise. See her essay: "Creating Organizational Change Without Positional Power," page 132.

What Does An Emergent Leader Organization Do?

As of 2015, 200 green building practitioners and advocates have participated in the two-day intensive EMERGE Leadership Workshop, with nearly 2,000 more attending seminars and presentations in California, Hawaii, Washington, and Oregon. These individuals work

Creating Organizational Change Without Positional Power

By <u>Meisha Rouser</u>, Organizational Psychologist, Doctoral Student, Leadership Studies

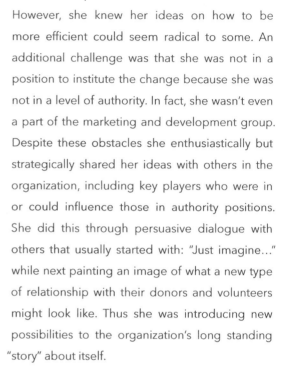

As anyone will know who has tried, creating change within an organization can be a complicated and frustrating process. This is especially true when you are not "positioned" to lead change in the organization. Robert Greenleaf believed that the servant-leader appropriately uses "persuasion" – which he defines as "gentle, non-judgmental argument" – to influence others to change (Greenleaf 2002, 43). In a commentary on Greenleaf's advice to persuade rather than coerce, David Rough defines persuasion as "a process of recruiting a willing partner(s) to accomplish a shared vision of purpose" (<u>Leadership Cache</u>, 2/10/11).

How can the emergent leader who has no positional power within an organization influence change?

Every organization has a story that holds in place its culture, its decision-making practices, its end goals. The first step for anyone wanting to influence from within is to understand the organization's story: what it is, how it came about, the mechanisms that maintain the story, and the structure the story maintains. The next step for the emergent leader might be to introduce ideas that are compatible with the current story, but move the organization forward to a more sustainable, emergent vision.

An example of this process comes from a non-profit organization I worked with. A member of the organization felt strongly that the organization needed to become more efficient and strategic in its marketing and development efforts.

However, she knew her ideas on how to be more efficient could seem radical to some. An additional challenge was that she was not in a position to institute the change because she was not in a level of authority. In fact, she wasn't even a part of the marketing and development group. Despite these obstacles she enthusiastically but strategically shared her ideas with others in the organization, including key players who were in or could influence those in authority positions. She did this through persuasive dialogue with others that usually started with: "Just imagine..." while next painting an image of what a new type of relationship with their donors and volunteers might look like. Thus she was introducing new possibilities to the organization's long standing "story" about itself.

It's important to note that these were dialogues. In addition to sharing her thoughts, she invited her conversational partners to contribute theirs, asking them, "What could this relationship look like? and "What's possible?" By liberally creating space for the interchange of ideas, she cultivated ownership of a possible change, and in the shaping of specific aspects of that change. After a short time, a small group came together including personnel at all levels of authority (from little to a lot) to pursue this new idea. This team eventually redefined the organization's marketing, advocacy, and development efforts. Our protagonist was not a member of the team, but she played an

Creating Organizational Change Without Positional Power *(Continued)*

important role in its formation and the eventual positive change that occurred in the organization's culture and effectiveness.

To help new ideas take shape and spread, pay attention to key words. As stated by Brian Robertson, author of Holacracy, The New Management System for a Rapidly Changing World, "language is commonly seen as the verbal expression of culture, but language can also create culture." One example Robertson uses is to avoid using the word "problem." He points out that humans tend to avoid dealing with "problems." The use of this word can create a "culture of avoidance or unnecessary trepidation." A problem exists when there is a difference (or gap) between reality and what was expected or hoped for. A more neutral word to describe this situation is "tension." Tension, and the process of working through the gap that is causing it, may not be comfortable. It does offer, however, the option of possibility and creation.

Many of the ideas in this book can be used to intervene within the systems an organization presents. However, one can start by planting the seeds of change through nurturing the development of a new story, encouraging input from others in its development, and celebrating the process. When the story evolves, and change results, wonderful things emerge. 🗲

---

in privately-run businesses, from small design firms serving local markets to large firms serving national and international markets and employing hundreds of thousands. They work for large urban municipalities, such as the City of Seattle and the City of Santa Monica, as well as medium-sized ones, such as the cities of Goleta, CA, and Bellevue and Edmonds, WA. They work for NGOs, such as the International Living Future Institute (ILFI), the regionally based Northwest EcoBuilding Guild, and Earth Advantage, and the more locally focused RePower Program in Kitsap County, WA.

In some cases, the organization's entire purpose is aligned with the ultimate goal of a sustainable built environment, as in the case of the ILFI, Global Green USA, or sustainable building consultancies such as O'Brien & Company in Seattle and Leading Edge Consulting in Los Angeles. In other cases, the organization includes sustainability as part of its mission or goal statements, as in the case of Jacobs Engineering, the City of Kirkland, WA, and Abode Communities (an affordable housing agency in the Los Angeles area). In either circumstance, these organizations fulfill the first criteria for an emergent leader organization. They are pursuing the goal to which emergent leadership aspires.

Regardless of what an organization's primary work is, it can do a tremendous service to us all if it champions transparency in the industry. See the sidebar, "Corporate Transparency," on page 134.

How Does an Emergent Leader Organization Work?

In doing its work, an emergent leader organization applies the same principles we have discussed that apply to an individual as an emergent leader. Does the organization serve its clients with the intent the client grows in understanding and capability to

Corporate Transparency

Emergent Leader Organizations can champion transparency in the industry. The ultimate goal of transparency initiatives is to transform markets. When the norm in the marketplace becomes transparency, those who have a vested interest in that market will not want to be seen as uncooperative, and will naturally want to be comfortable with what they are being asked to reveal. Although they are the lion's share of the green building movement's drive for transparency, product ingredient listings and "green" building product certifications – including when the "product" is a building! – are only part of an expanding transparency initiative within the green building movement. Corporate social responsibility is another, and many companies are choosing to release CSR reports that include data about what they have accomplished in this regard. Relevant to green building, there are a couple of opportunities for taking this step toward greater transparency: The JUST label released by the ILFI at GreenBuild in the fall of 2013, which focuses on increasing social justice; and the AIA 2030 Commitment, which focuses on reducing energy consumption and associated CO_2 emissions.

Organizations of all types and sizes can earn the JUST label when they are willing to report on 22 social and equity indicators related to six categories: diversity, equity, safety, worker benefit, local benefit, and stewardship. Like the ILFI's DECLARE label – which applies to product manufacturing – the JUST labeling process is voluntary. JUST isn't merely a means of determining how well you are doing. It can help businesses and other organizations become mindful of the way they lead, and to what they are aspiring. Just as with building certification processes, the JUST self-assessment process can illuminate the gap or tension between where an organization is and where the organization would like to be. It's a learning process.

As the name implies, the AIA 2030 Commitment is designed expressly for AIA's membership. Member firms participating in the 2030 Commitment have agreed to measure and share information about the energy performance of the buildings they design as well as the energy they (the members) consume to operate their design practice. More than 300 firms, including several represented by EMERGE Alumni, are participating. As faculty for the AIA 2030 Professional Seminar Series in Seattle (now online nationally), I heard two early signatories to the commitment, DLR and Miller Hull Partnership, openly present what and how they were doing to members of other firms. This is transparency at its best. And you can bet that there were many individuals in the audience were wondering how they could get their firms to sign on.

An emergent leader organization is willing to share information for the greater good and participates in these corporate transparency initiatives.

Note: This sidebar is an excerpt/adaptation from my post "How transparency can change the game on green building" to DJC Green Building Blog, February 27, 2014) ❧

implement sustainable building goals? In other words, is the organization applying the principle of servant leadership? When I was a full-time sustainability consultant, my explicit promise to clients when making a proposal was: "At the conclusion of this project, if your company, community, organization does not have a greater capacity to act in accordance with sustainability principles, than I have failed as your consultant."

Does the organization fully understand that its intention regarding greater sustainability asks those they serve to adopt change? Is the organization willing to work with its employees and its clients to help them fully understand the implication of their decisions, and the value of decisions that might lead towards the ultimate vision of a truly sustainable built environment? To show how these decisions are in alignment with its overall purpose as an organization and as good citizens? To build confidence that the actions informed by these decisions can make a real difference? If we as advocates of sustainability are asking others to invest time, energy, talent, and dollars in the effort, the organizations we lead should do so by example.

Emergent leader organizations understand the importance of collaborative learning and implementation in achieving long-lasting change. When planning meetings, discussions, and project events, they research attitudes toward and experience with the envisioned end goal, provide resources, engage the full spectrum of all those involved and to be impacted, and exhibit caring for the results. They employ an integrated process in designing solutions, whether those solutions are brick and mortar, community policies, or affordable housing programs. Rather than rely on lock-step public process minimums, emergent leader organizations go the extra mile with the resources available. Emergent leader organizations model creativity in the way they approach problems, and in the solutions that evolve through their efforts.

Finally, a client, customer, employee, or colleague of an emergent leader organization should feel cared for. It's not just a job or even just a cause. An emergent leader organization extends its welcome and invites you into a larger community of people hoping to make the world a better place for this generation and the next, and so on.

How Does an Emergent Leader Organization Operate?

In his classic lecture "Creativity and Leadership in Learning Communities," Fritjof Capra notes: "[i]n human organizations, both [emergent and designed] types of structures are always present. The designed structures are the organization's formal structures, which are depicted in its official documents and describe the organization's mission, its formal policies, its strategies, and so on. In addition, there are always emergent structures. There are the organization's informal structures – the alliances and friendships, the informal channels of communication (the grapevine), the tacit skills and sources of knowledge that are continually evolving. These structures emerge from an informal network of relationships that continually grows, changes, and adapts to new situations."

Capra goes on to discuss how important it is to maintain order without lapsing into rigidity and to maintain creativity without lapsing into chaos. He writes, "The challenge for any organization is to find a creative balance between its designed structures and its emergent structures" (Capra 1997, 7-8). Capra's advice is useful, regardless of whether the formal structure of the given organization would be considered more or less aligned with the goal of sustainability. How does one facilitate emergence? According to Capra, "[b]y creating a learning culture; by continually questioning and rewarding innovation; by building up and nurturing a network of learning conversations; by creating an environment of support, trust, and respect, and by allowing experimentation and the freedom to make mistakes" (Capra 1997, 9). He encourages us to develop a leadership that "would be a facilitation of emergence. This type of leadership is not limited to a single individual." He compares it to a "self-organizing system, in which leadership is distributed, and responsibility becomes a capacity of the whole" (Capra 1997, 8).

In *Leadership and the New Science*, Wheatley tells us that "new information can disturb a system to the point it self-organizes to a higher level of complexity, [becoming] a better version of itself" (Wheatley 2006, 87).

Creating an Emergent "Designed Structure"

Capra invites us to think about how emergence can be facilitated throughout an organization. Thus even the "designed structure" he refers to can reflect emergence. In *Holacracy*, Brian Robertson, presents a form of organizational structure that responds to Capra's invitation. He defines *holacracy* as a "new social technology for governing and operating an organization" (Robertson 2015, 12), one in which the "core authority structure and processes of an organization fundamentally hold space for everyone to have and use power, and do not allow anyone – even a leader – to co-opt the power of others" (Robertson 2015, 21).

Every organization is challenged by "tensions" due to the "human capacity to sense dissonance in the present moment and to see the potential for change" (Robertson 2015, 5). Robertson invites organizations to see this as an opportunity rather than a problem. He also believes that organizational structure can get in the way from truly leveraging this opportunity. He asks, "How can we make an organization not just evolved but evolutionary…, one that can sense and adapt and learn and integrate?" (Robertson 2015, 7). When tensions can be processed quickly and effectively, the organization (and the organization's work) can "benefit from an enhanced capacity to dynamically and continually evolve" (Robertson 2015, 7).

Robertson believes that conventional organizations are not designed to rapidly evolve. Even if they perceive the benefit of learning and evolving, the opportunity to do so is lost. "At best, the novel techniques become a 'bolt-on' – something that affects just one aspect of the organization and remains in continual conflict with the other systems around it…. At worst, the 'corporate antibodies' come out and reject the bolted-on techniques" (Robertson 2015, 10).

Robertson has designed an evolutionary and intriguing model of business organization. The elements include "a constitution, which sets out the 'rules of the game' and redistributes authority, a…way to structure an organization and define people's roles and spheres of authority within it, a…decision-making process for updating those roles and authorities, and a meeting process for keeping teams in sync and getting work done together" (Robertson 2015, 12).

Robertson notes that *holacracy* is "just one example of a system that uses peer-to-peer self organization and distributes control in lieu of more traditional approaches to achieving order" (Robertson 2015, 203). Evolution "seems to favor processes that allow peer-to-peer, emergent order to show up in response to real tensions…; when you have a system that distributes authority and honors the autonomy of all its parts and players, you also get a system capable of acting more as a cohesive integrated whole at the same time" (Robertson 2015, 204). If you lead an organization, or you are willing to consider re-organizing your conventionally structured business, Robertson's book is definitely worth a read. The Holacracy website provides resources to get you started, including a constitution template.

Robertson does not seem to be suggesting a change in corporate legal structure. In the case of businesses that wish not only to evolve but to promote a social benefit such as sustainability, however, this might be a good idea. The legalization of social-purpose or certified benefit (B Corp) business structures means corporations can now prioritize aspirations such as, for example, environmental protection and social justice, without risking the ire and potential legal hazards of profit-minded shareholders. ("Social Purpose Corporation" June 15, 2015) Neil Kelly Company, a residential design-build remodeling business heavily committed to green building practice, became a B Corp in 2013. According to the company's declaration on B Corp's website: Neil Kelly works "to benefit our people, our planet and our profit – in that order. We are committed to our community and our environment. We *became a B Corporation to 'walk our talk'. By constructing our values into the legal backbone of our company, we'll ensure they will never be compromised for generations to come*" (B Corp Community, April 29, 2015).

Where social-purpose or certified benefit *(B Corp)* structures are not an option, becoming a co-operative might be. Third Place Design Co-operative, founded by EMERGE workshop alumna Poppi Handy, is the first for-profit design co-operative in Washington State, and one of very few in the country. (See "Transformation in Practice: Third Place Design Co-op," page 139.)

I am sure that most readers work for or own businesses with conventional legal structures. O'Brien & Company (without me now since 2011) is a conventionally structured corporation closing in on its 25th year. There are principals-in-charge with decision authority; however, the firm maintains a fairly flat organizational model with teams operating and co-operating around the corporation's mission. Each team has both financial and mission-based goals feeding into the larger vision of the company and long-time health.

When the firm moved to Seattle in 2006, our tenant improvement project was one of the first to showcase LEED Gold for Commercial Interiors. It frequently shares information with other organizations about aspects of its operation, including for example how that TI project was conducted, and how the firm successfully managed the transition resulting from my retirement. The firm has held an annual retreat since its inception (even when it was just me!), and I'm told staff members are more and more directly involved in planning and creating the retreat experience and developing team work plans and targets. Notably, the firm has won several *Seattle Times* People's Pick awards for "Favorite Green Collar Company." It maintains a reputation for hard work, good service, and quality results, reflected in the national and regional awards its accrued for client projects, loyal client base, and little staff turnover – all while holding itself to its mission of sustainability. So even when coloring within the lines of a legal corporate structure, there is much you can do.

In considering how your organization measures against the ideal of emergent leadership, ask these questions:

Does the organization incorporate servant leadership in its approach to internal management? Again, this leadership approach means a steadfast commitment to growing all those led into leaders who in turn wish to serve. By providing its staff copies of Kent Keith's *"The Case for Servant Leadership,"* and also *"The Seven Pillars of Servant Leadership"* when that resource became available, and holding discussions on the topic at staff retreats, we at O'Brien & Company were challenging ourselves to meet this standard.

Does the organization support professional leadership development? Is there an explicit mentoring program in place? Are all members of the staff involved in creating in-house educational opportunities? At the Third Place Cooperative, all members are resources for each other; they also see themselves as an educational resource for the design community.

Does the organization foster community internally, through opportunities to play, learn, and dialogue on meaningful topics? Are members of the organization recognized for their work in the larger community, and are they encouraged to do such work?

How to Become an Emergent Leader Organization: The First Step

It is likely that the organization you are involved in cannot answer "yes" to all of the questions above. Or you feel it might be able to say "yes," but could do better – which is probably true for most of us. One of the first steps for an organization aspiring to be an emergent leader organization is to develop "self-awareness." Just as I stress the importance of assessing your own personal attitudes, abilities, and actions when setting out to become an emergent leader, an organization needs to know where it lands in terms of its purpose, policies, and practice. The practice of witnessing is just as applicable here. And rather than blaming the organization for what it isn't, it will be important to understand what it is! This understanding implies reflection and thoughtful dialogue about what it could be. An organization is as emergent as its members - *all of them* - aspire it to be.

TRANSFORMATION IN PRACTICE:
Third Place Design Co-operative

In late March, 2015 I facilitated Third Place Design Co-operative's first organizational retreat. In addition to founder Poppi Handy (2nd to left in photo), TPDC at the time included (from L. to R.): Leticia Lucero, Suzanne Davis, Brent Chastain, and Benjamin Maestas. The co-operative was in its formative stages; several in the group were quite new to the organization. The purpose of the retreat

was three-fold: "1) To connect with each other, build a team, become a family; 2) To know who we are as a co-operative, and how we will present ourselves to the world; and 3) To begin to understand what it means for us to function as the co-operative and business we want to be day-to-day, and what this might take." The theme for the retreat was *Emergence*.

TPDC acts as a unique exemplar to others seeking to create emergent organizations in the sustainability field, first in its decision to be a for-profit co-operative, and second in its commitment to instituting meaningful mechanisms to learn, evolve, and lead - evidenced by the unusual investment in a three-day off-site retreat of the entire staff so early in the process of formation.

When Poppi and I discussed plans for the retreat, she shared the draft by-laws and articles of incorporation with me, as well as the fact that she had considered forming a B-Corp or social purpose corporation, but was drawn to the more democratic form of a co-op. Washington Law does not permit businesses to be both a social purpose corporation and a co-operative, so she chose the latter. This option did mean that "TPDC needed to get a special ruling from the Attorney General's office to be both a for-profit and a co-operative, as Washington State law is contradictory in its language when applying for both of these statuses" (Handy August 7, 2015).

TPDC's articles of incorporation do include, however, language in its Article 3 that you might see with a B-Corp, to wit:

"Third Place Design Co-operative Inc. is organized to provide architectural services in a manner intended to promote positive effects and minimize adverse effects of its activities upon 1) the corporation's employees, suppliers, and customers; 2) the local, state, national, or world community; and 3) the environment.

The mission of Third Place Design Co-operative Inc. is to promote social and environmental equality in the communities in which we design structures, administer the building of structures and implement our ideas.

The mission of Third Place Design Co-operative Inc. is not necessarily compatible with and may be contrary to maximizing profits and earnings for shareholders, or maximizing shareholder value in any sale, merger, acquisition, or other similar action of the corporation." (TPDC, 2015)

One of the commitments one makes as part of the firm and as a co-op (to themselves and to the national and international co-operative community) is to share lessons learned with the world, so that others hoping to form co-operatives might benefit. This is very much in character with emergent leadership, where one hopes to foster others to learn and lead, and which requires a transparency unheard of in conventional business ventures.

The desire for transparency was apparent throughout the retreat. In addition to the opportunity to socialize over meals, games, and during unscheduled time, the retreat provided an opportunity to both look at what they as individuals and a group bring to the table today in terms of skills, attributes, and desires, and what possibilities these could invoke in building a successful business. Naturally, one of the concerns included how to function within the constraints of a design practice and the intrinsic hierarchy that entails, while maintaining and expanding a cooperative identity. Conversations over the weekend were frank, thoughtful, and productive. Keeping up with the conversation meant running multiple flip charts at a time! Discussions ranged from large-picture topics, such as their purpose, to more detailed topics, such as what services (paid and otherwise) they could comfortably offer to fulfill this purpose. The mood was often serious, and just as often silly. While many business retreats produce five-year plans, and in this case a 90-day plan to kick-start the effort, very few have been created with the deep commitment and ownership that I witnessed during the retreat.

TPDC's Five Big Goals include: "1) Provide a space and advocacy that nurtures and strengthens community; 2) Experience resiliency through financial stability.; 3) Develop a common understanding of office processes, policies, and practices; 4) 80% of our projects will support our mission; and 5) Provide an environment that nurtures and supports a healthy and balanced lifestyle for ourselves." These goals inform all of their planning.

When I visited the crew in their offices, July, 2015, they had grown by one, recent architectural program graduate Jenny Prieto. Jenny actually provided an answer to the question: "Could the energy and intellectual capital cultivated at the retreat be passed on to new members of the co-op?"

The unanimous answer (and perhaps more importantly Jenny's answer) was "Yes!" Two months in, Jenny had had the opportunity to work with each member of the organization, getting to know them and learning technical skills from them. And like all staff, she participates in a weekly meeting where all topics are on the table.

The five-year plan developed at the retreat acts as a rudder for the staff meeting, so all items (whether it's deadlines, an upcoming camping trip, or office supplies) are discussed in terms of the moving the plan forward. The 5-point 90-day plan was front-and-center as well. (They reported that 4 out of 5 items had been achieved in the 90-day window. Major thumbs up!) For the original 90-day plan, each firm member took responsibility for being the "lead" on one of each of the five points. Notably, when I met with them, Jenny had already proposed to take the lead on an idea for the next 90-day plan that is in keeping with Goals 1 and 5 of their Five Year: *to coordinate a volunteer project.*

Since this is Jenny's first job as a design professional, she "doesn't know any other way!" (Prieto July 23, 2015.) Poppi, however, shared how in her former experience, the kinds of things discussed at TPDC meetings were "rarely talked about, even at the partnership level" (Handy July 23, 2015).

And the promise to share the evolutionary story of TPDC is not empty. In addition to being willing to be a case study for this book, I learned at our lunch meeting that both the five-year plan goals and the 90-day task list were posted for all to see at the firm's first open house. Says firm member Leticia, "The purpose of doing this was to allow conversation with our guests on these issues. [Explaining ourselves] had the added benefit of helping us 'own' our business practice and our history. Honestly, there were times as a newer member I didn't have an answer to some of the questions our visitors were asking, but listening to Poppi respond to questions provided perspective that I could then relay to those questioning me" (Lucero August 6, 2015).

Most tellingly, everyone at TPDC owns the vision and the plan. Says newest member Jenny: "I believe in this firm, in this co-op, and I believe in the 90-day and 5-year plan. I know everyone at the firm believes in what we are doing and why we are here. I think it's important to communicate to your readers that there is a true commitment and huge 'I believe' factor at work here" (Prieto August 6, 2015).

References

American Institute of Architects (AIA). 2008. *Contracts Documents: Integrated Project Delivery (IPD) Family.* http://acdpages.aia.org/IPDGuide.html. Last retrieved August 24, 2015.

American National Standards Institute (ANSI). 2012. "ANSI IP Standard 2.0. http://webstore.ansi.org. Last retrieved August 24, 2015.

Architecture 2030. 2015. "The 2030 Challenge for Planning." http://architecture2030.org/2030_challenges/2030_challenge_planning/. Last retrieved September 2, 2015.

Aubrey, Bob and Paul Cohen. 1995. *Working Wisdom: Timeless Skills and Vanguard Strategies for Learning Organizations.* San Francisco, CA: Jossey Bass.

BCorporation.Net. April 29, 2015. "Neil Kelly." http://www.bcorporation.net/community/neil-kelly-company.

Brown, Stuart. 2009. *Play: How it Shapes the Brain.* New York, NY: Penguin Group.

Brown, Ted. May 2008. "Tales of Creativity and Play" TED Talk at the Serious Play Conference, http://www.ted.com/talks/tim_brown_on_creativity_and_play?language=en. Last retrieved September 8, 2015.

Bullitt Center. Jan. 11, 2013. "Living Proof: Building the Bullitt Center." http://bullittcenter.org. Last retrieved June 30, 2015. (Article retired.)

Campanelli, Joe. July 2015. Campanelli Construction. Phone.

Capra, Fritjof. April 18, 1997. "Creativity and Leadership in Learning Communities," a lecture to the Mill Valley School District, Published by the Center for EcoLiteracy, Berkeley, CA. http://nextreformation.com/wp-admin/resources/creativity.pdf. Last retrieved August 24, 2015.

Cialdini, Robert. 2007. *Influence: The Psychology of Persuasion*, New York, NY: Harper Collins.

City of Seattle. April 2014. "Data as of April 1, 2013, an April 2, 2014." https://performance.seattle.gov/Government/Energy-Benchmarking-Compliance-Rates/4cdr-g5h6. Last retrieved August 20, 2015.

City of Seattle Department of Planning and Development and Weber Thompson. December 31, 2011. *South Lake Union Urban Design Framework.* http://www.seattle.gov/dpd/cs/groups/pan/@pan/documents/web_informational/dpds021898.pdf. Last retrieved June 11, 2015.

"Cognitive reframing," October 2014. Wikipedia. https://en.wikipedia.org/wiki/Cognitive_reframing. Last retrieved June 20, 2015.

Combe, Matthew. August 17, 2015. Seattle 2030 District. Phone.

Daley-Peng, Nora. February 8, 2011. "Clarifying the Integrative Design Process: Ansi Standard Gets an Overhaul With IP Version 2.0." http://www.obrienandco.com/clarifying-the-integrative-design-process-ansi-standard-gets-an-overhaul-with-ip-version-20/. Last retrieved August 24, 2015.

Doppelt, Bob. 2008. *The Power of Sustainable Thinking: How to Create a Positive Future for the Climate, the Planet, Your Organization, and Your Life.* Sterling, VA: Earthscan.

Eggers, Krista. August 13, 2015. Enterprise Community Partners. Phone.

Ehrenfeld, John. June 11, 2015. www.johnehrenfeld.com/index.shtml.

Enterprise Community Partners. 2015. "Our Story." http://www.enterprisecommunity.com/servlet/servlet.FileDownload?file=00P3000000C8vbVEAR. Last retrieved August 14, 2015.

Faul, Angela. June 5, 2013. ACKJ Consulting. Phone.

Greenleaf, Robert. 2002. "The Servant as Leader." From the 25th edition of *Servant Leadership: A Journey into the Nature of Legitimate Power & Greatness.* Mahwah, NJ: Paulist Press.

Handy, Poppi. July 23, 2015. Third Place Design Cooperative. Meeting.

Handy, Poppi. August 7, 2015. Third Place Design Cooperative. Email.

Heath, Chip and Dan Heath. 2010. *Switch: How To Change Things When Change Is Hard.* New York, NY: Broadway/Crown Publishing.

Hosey, Lance. 2013. "Keynote, Government Confluence." Seattle, WA: International Living Future Institute.

Jackson, Alistair. July 30, 2015. O'Brien & Company. Email.

Jackson, Alistair. August 8, 2015. O'Brien & Company. Email.

Kahane, Adam. 2012. *Transformative Scenario Planning*. San Francisco, CA: Berrett-Koehler.

Kahn, Brad. July 2, 2015. Groundwork Strategies. Email.

Kania, John and Mark Kramer. January 21, 2013. "Embracing Emergence: How Collective Impact Addresses Complexity," *Stanford Social Innovation Review*. http://ssir.org/articles/entry/embracing_emergence_how_collective_impact_addresses_complexity. Last retrieved July 9, 2015.

Keith, Kent M. 2008. *The Case for Servant Leadership*. Westfield, IN: The Greenleaf Center for Servant Leadership.

Knecht, Eric. August 3, 2015. Resources for Community Development. Phone.

Kouzes, James and Barry Posner. 2007. *The Leadership Challenge, 4th Ed*. San Francisco, CA: Jossey-Bass/Wiley.

_____. 2003. *Credibility*. San Francisco, CA: Jossey-Bass/Wiley.

Lean Construction Institute. July 15, 2015. "Glossary." http://www.leanconstruction.org/training/glossary/#p. Last retrieved December 31, 2015.

Lennick, Doug and Fred Kiel. 2005. *Moral Intelligence*. Upper Saddle River, NJ: Pearson Education/ Wharton School Publishing.

Liedtka, Jeanne and Henry Mintzberg. 2013. "Time for Design," *Rotman on Design*. Toronto, CA: University of Toronto Press.

Lucero, Leticia. August 6, 2015. Third Place Design Cooperative. Email.

Macy, Joanna and Chris Johnstone. 2012. *Active Hope: How to Face the Mess We're in Without Going Crazy.* Novato, CA: New World Library.

Malin, Nadav. 2005. "The Mindset Thing: Exploring the Deeper Potential of Integrated Design," Brattleboro, VT: Environmental Building News. Available at: http://www.integrativedesign.net/images/MindsetThing.pdf. Last retrieved from BuildingGreen.com, July 2, 2015.

Marquez-Brookes, Maria Elena. April 6, 2011. As quoted in "Green Resident Engagement Cards Inform and Empower in California Non-Profit Housing Developments." http://www.obrienandco.com/green-resident-engagement-cards-inform-and-empower-in-california-non-profit-housing-developments-interview-with-maria-elen/. Last retrieved August 15, 2015.

Martin, Roger (editor), and Karen Christensen (editor). 2013. *Rotman on Design: The Best on Design Thinking from Rotman Magazine.* Toronto, ONT: University of Toronto Press, Scholarly Publishing Division, 2013.

McGonigal, Kelly. 2011. *The Willpower Instinct.* New York, NY: Penguin Group.

Meadows, Donella. 2008. *Thinking in Systems: A Primer.* Chelsea Green Publishing.

_____. 1999. "Leverage Points: Places to Intervene in a System." Donella Meadows Institute. http://www.donellameadows.org/archives/leverage-points-places-to-intervene-in-a-system/. Last retrieved July 12, 2015.

_____. 2006. (Posthumously, Ed. Diana Wright) *Thinking in Systems.* White River Junction, VT: Chelsea Green Publishing.

Meadows, Donella, Dennis Meadows and Jorgen Randers. 1992. *"Beyond the Limits to Growth,"* Back Issue Library of *In Context*. https://digital.lib.washington.edu/dspace-law/bitstream/handle/1773.1/1300/3WJELP125.pdf?sequence=1. Last retrieved June 11, 2015.

Meadows, Dennis and Linda Booth Sweeney. 1995. *The Systems Thinking Playbook*. White River Junction, VT: Chelsea Green Publishing.

Meyer, Rachael. July, 2013. Berger Partnership. Phone.

Meyer, Rachael. July 23-24, 2015. Berger Partnership. Emails.

Nhat Hanh, Thich. 1998. *Teachings on Love*. Berkeley, CA: Parallax Press.

National Commission on the Environment. 1993. "Choosing a Sustainable Future: The Report of the National Commission on the Environment." Washington, DC: Island Press.

O'Brien, Kathleen. August 1, 2013. "New Trim Tab: Exploring the Place of Leadership and the Leadership of Place." Building Capacity (Blog) http://buildingcapacity.typepad.com/blog/living-building-challenge/. Last retrieved November 7, 2015.

O'Brien, Kathleen, Nicole DeNamur and Elizabeth Powers. November, 2013. "Legal Hurdles Faced by Deep Green Buildings: Case Studies and Recommendations." Washington Journal of Environmental Law & Policy, Volume 3, Issue 2. Seattle, WA: UW School of Law. https://digital.lib.washington.edu/dspace-law/bitstream/handle/1773.1/1300/3WJELP125.pdf?sequence=1. Last retrieved June 11, 2015.

Perry, Imani with Krista Tippett. September 11, 2014. "The Fabric of
Our Identity." *http://www.onbeing.org/program/imani-perry-
the-fabric-of-our-identity/transcript/6758*. Last retrieved August
24, 2015.

Positive Psychology Resources. 2014. "Flexible Optimism."
http://www.centreforconfidence.co.uk/pp/overview.
php?p=c2lkPTQmdGlkPTAmaWQ9NjE. Last retrieved
September 6, 2015.

Prieto, Jenny. July 23, 2015. Third Place Design Cooperative. Meeting.

Prieto, Jenny. August 6, 2015. Third Place Cooperative. Email.

Prochaska, James, John Norcross and Carlo Diclemente. 2006.
*Changing for Good: A Revolutionary Six-Stage Program
for Overcoming Bad Habits and Moving Your Life Positively
Forward.* New York: Harper Collins.

Reed William. June 11, 2013. Regenesis. Email.

Robertson, Brian J. 2015. *Holacracy: The New Management System
for a Rapidly Changing World.* New York, NY: Henry Holt
and Co.

"Sangha," July 10, 2015. Wikipedia. https://en.wikipedia.org/wiki/
Sangha. Last retrieved August 6, 2015.

Scharmer, Otto. 2009. *Theory U: Leading from the Future as it
Emerges.* San Francisco, CA: Berrett-Koehler Publishers.

Scharmer, Otto and Katrin Kaufer. 2013. *Leading from the Emerging
Future: From Ego-System to EcoSystem Economics.* San
Francisco, CA: Berrett-Koehler Publishers.

Seattle 2030 District. 2013. "Leading Change: 2013 Annual Report." http://www.2030districts.org/sites/default/files/atoms/files/2030.Report.2013.pdf. Last retrieved August 20, 2015.

Seattle 2030 District. 2015. "Seattle 2030 District Strategic Plan." http://www.2030districts.org/sites/default/files/atoms/files/Seattle_2030_District_Strategic_Plan.pdf. Last retrieved August 20, 2015.

Seligman, Martin. 2011. *Flourish.* New York, NY: Free Press.

7Group and Bill Reed. 2009. *The Integrative Design Guide to Green Building.* Hoboken, NJ: Wiley.

Sipe, James and Don Frick. 2009. *Seven Pillars of Servant Leadership.* Mahway, NJ: Paulist Press.

"Social Purpose Corporation," June 15, 2015. Wikipedia. https://en.wikipedia.org/wiki/Social_purpose_corporation. Last retrieved September 7, 2015.

Spears, Larry. 1995. "Introduction: Servant-Leadership and The Greenleaf Legacy." From *Reflections on Leadership.* New York, NY: John Wiley & Sons.

The Natural Step. August 21, 2015. "What is Backcasting?" http://www.thenaturalstep.org/sustainability/backcasting/.

Third Place Design Cooperative (TPDC). March 2015. "Articles of Incorporation," Draft. Provided by Poppi Handy, TPDC.

United Nations World Commission on Economic Development (Widely known as the "Brundtland Commission"). 1987. "Report of the World Commission on Economic Development: Our Common Future." http://www.un-documents.net/our-common-future.pdf. Last retrieved June 11, 2015.

U.S. Green Building Council. October 20, 2014. Available at http://www.usgbc.org/resources/integrative-process-worksheet. Last retrieved August 24, 2015.

Urban Environmental Institute. 2002. *Resource Guide for Sustainable Design in an Urban Environment*, 2002. http://issuu.com/mithun/docs/slu_final_10-22-02/73. Last retrieved June 11, 2015.

Wheatley, Margaret. 2006. *Leadership and the New Science*, 3rd Ed. San Francisco, CA: Berrett-Koehler.

Appendix

1. Self-Evaluation

Do you know your purpose (the 'business you are in')? How would you describe it?

Why do you want to be a leader in the context of sustainability of the built environment?

In your own words, where are you in your adult development? Would you say you are dependent, independent, or interdependent in most of your relationships with others?

In your own words, where are you in your leadership development? Would you say you are a (benevolent) autocrat, manager/leader, collaborative/leader, servant leader, or emergent leader in most of your interactions with those you lead?

_____

_____

_____

_____

In decision-making processes, where do you most frequently find yourself? Why do you think this is so?

Mandate	Coercive	Persuasive	Consultative	Consensus

_____

_____

_____

_____

How does this style of decision-making match your goals? How effective has it been?

_____

_____

_____

_____

How well do you exhibit the following characteristics of a "credible" leader?
*   Do you do what you say you will do? Are you honest?
*   Do you think ahead for the greater good?
*   Do you act from competence? In other words, do you know what you are doing?
*   Are you positive and encouraging?
*   Can you detach from specific outcomes if the direction is in the "right direction?"

Do you remember an instance in which you behaved like the leader you'd like to be? Describe the emotional, cognitive, and/or spiritual state you were in at the time*, and what you actually did? (*Ask yourself: "How was I feeling? What was I thinking? What was my intention?")

Do you remember an instance in which you did NOT behave like the leader you'd like to be? Describe the emotional, cognitive, and/or spiritual state you were in at the time*, and what you actually did? (*Ask yourself: "How was I feeling? What was I thinking? What was my intention?")

What leadership challenge(s) seems to recur frequently for you?

What are the strengths you naturally bring to leadership?

What leadership attributes are you particularly interested in developing or improving? (Keep in mind the attributes of an emergent leader.)

_____

_____

_____

_____

What do you think you need to do to grow to the next stage of development?

_____

_____

_____

_____

If applying best practices, what would it look like when that recurring leadership challenge comes up the next time?

_____

_____

_____

_____

.

2. Leadership Focus

In which context(s) do you wish to lead? (Personal, Organization, Community) Describe **what** your leadership in these context(s) could look like, **who** it is you are hoping to lead/ influence, and the desired **outcome**?

Leadership Context	What	Who	Outcome
Personal			
Organizational			
Community			

Where are these individuals/groups you hope to lead/influence on the attitudinal spectrum of change towards the desired outcome? You can use the table below to visually plot the landscape you will be working with/within.

Contexts	Disinterest	Deliberating	Designing	Doing	Defending
Personal					
Organizational					
Community					

3. Personal Leadership Skills Development Plan

In the next 6 months, what will you do to "grow" your leadership capacity in the emotional, cognitive, and spiritual realms, keeping in mind your leadership focus? Focus on areas of strength as well as of need. Activities can include studying, practicing, reflecting, and/ or sharing. They can be individual or with supportive communities. The matrix is provided as a guideline, not a "fence." **Just ignore lines when they get in the way.** A single activity might combine emotion (feeling), cognition (thinking), and/or spirit (acting). For example, if you make a plan to regularly review your day for feelings, thoughts, and works, this "practice" feeds all three areas of personal development.

* An example of **study** might be reading a book on servant leadership, dispassionately conducting a daily inventory of feelings, thoughts, and works, or joining/creating a support group studying a pertinent theme.
* An example of **practice** might be physical integration, a simple daily spiritual practice incorporating the service theme, unconditional or anonymous acts of service, or mentoring an individual who is struggling with an issue you've dealt with in the past.
* An example of **reflection** would include journaling or quiet contemplation.
* An example of **sharing** would be making a point of sharing insights from your personal investigation with your colleagues, clients, and family, creating in-service mini-workshops on leadership topics and your emerge leadership learnings, posting on the EL Alumni Linked-In Site, or writing a guest article on the Emerge Leadership blog.

	Study	Practice	Reflection	Sharing
Emotional: How do I build my emotional intelligence?				
Cognitive: How do I build my cognitive intelligence?				
Spiritual: How do I build my spiritual intelligence?				

4. 90-Day Action Plan

Create a 90-day action plan to begin working on your personal leadership development and make progress on your leadership focus. Identify peers and mentors who could act as allies in implementing your 90-day action plan. Remember your 90-day plan action goals should be: few in number (5-7 max), actionable (duh), attainable, accounted for (someone else knows you have accomplished it), bound in time, and prioritized (in order of importance). Include a commitment to celebrate in a specific way upon satisfactory performance of your plan.

Actions:

1. _____

2. _____

3. _____

4. _____

5. _____

Allies: _____

Celebration: _____

Acknowledgments

First, thanks to all in the EMERGE Leadership Community – Faculty, Alumni, Board Members, Sponsors, and Program Partners – who have encouraged me to write this book. Both in words and through your inspirational dedication to the ultimate goal of a life-sustaining built environment your commitment to lead the effort. Similar gratitude to all in the worldwide sustainable building community; for decades you have persevered and your work has made the world a better place.

Special thanks to my husband, John, sons Chris and Scott, granddaughter Ellie, and Friends who have helped with supportive phone calls, texts, emoticons, and coffee therapy when the going got rough; if you've written a book, you know the going got rough.

For that reason, it was especially good that I had a powerful team behind me to produce this book: editors Evyan Horton and David Kragen, designers Suzanne Davis and Hillary Handy, and dynamo consultant to New Hope Press, Trudy Catterfeld. A shout out to Corbet Corfman who designed the original EMERGE logo that everyone just loves. He also developed the graphics illustrating the EMERGE Leadership Model as well as the Sustainability Spiral that we use in the workshops and throughout this book. Berger Partnership developed the Emergent Collaboration Graphics featured in many of our seminars and in the book (Chapter 11.) Meanwhile, thanks to all the others who have contributed graphics and intel for our case studies. A special thanks to colleagues Elizabeth Powers, Molly McCabe, Ann Edminster,

Bill Reed, and Meisha Rouser for taking time out of their busy lives to write thoughtful essays to enrich the text.

Finally, thanks to Mom and Dad, who didn't get to see this book (Dad you almost did!) but made it very clear that my purpose in life was to learn something and do some good with what I learned.

Author's Final Note

My *hope* is for this book to assist you on your personal leadership journey, with the ultimate goal of making this world a better place for all living species, now and into the future. My *goal* for this book is that it be a living guide, one that continues to serve in a timely manner. With that in mind, the EMERGE Leadership Project has dedicated a significant portion of its website real estate to providing additional enrichment resources that can be updated and enhanced. This information is available to anyone who has purchased the book OR borrowed it from your local library, or read it and suggested your local library purchase it! If you meet these qualifications -- honor system only -- feel free to access the Book Bonus Materials at www.emergeleadershipthebook.org. You'll be asked to enter a password: EMERGEBkPlus.

Here's what you will find:

1. **Chapter Enrichment Resources:** This includes exercises that will help you reflect on the concepts described in a particular chapter and how it might apply in your personal leadership journey. It also includes links to videos and recorded Power-Points that align with the particular chapter. (The videos were recorded for an on-line educational platform in 2013.)

2. **Links:** EMERGE (the book) contains many hyperlinks for individuals or organizations you might be curious about. If you have purchased the e-book version, you can click on these

links. If you have purchased the print on demand version, you can access a link library in this password protected section of the website.

3. **Good Reads:** There is a publicly available "resource" section on website. Good reads, however, includes a bibliography of my favorite reads aligned with book chapters, and is likely to include resources not found in the generally available resource center.

As noted in the preface, I would love to hear about your leadership work. In addition to the contact information provided in the preface, you can find me on LinkedIn and Facebook. Let's connect! Best wishes on your journey.